Love's Cauld

Invites those who feel a deep calling to:

- Celebrate your sensitivity as a powerful gift
- Reawaken your wild, feminine, and untamed essence
- Express your true self with confidence and grace
- Resonate with the magic of the natural world
- Embrace a nature-centered perspective
- Recognize and release self-limiting beliefs
- Free yourself from the constraints of societal expectations
- Trust your creativity, intuition, and inner wisdom
- Claim the part of you that is a witch
- Realize the essential role of the divine feminine in balancing and sustaining our world
- Recognize and honor the non-human world

✹

This book is an invitation to reclaim
the sacred power of the divine feminine
that lives within you.

Praise for Love's Cauldron

In this beautiful testament to natural magic, Lehr artfully interweaves myth, personal story and poetic incantation to offer essential feminine medicine for our parched postmodern world. Vital nourishment and inspiration await in these pages for all who seek ripe seeds, fresh sparks and essential openings on the path of transformation.

~Shelly Eyre Graham, PhD, Clinical Psychologist & Author

Lehr takes us on a magical journey in *"Love's Cauldron"*, recounting her own history of vulnerabilities, exploration, and ultimate empowerment, as she traces her evolution into the wisdom of the witch. She explains methods of divination to commune with spirit guides, the power of tapping into the hidden forces of Nature, and the potency of spiritual embodiment. The informative text, interspersed with stream-of-consciousness musings and evocative poetry, serves as a guide for the reader to access their own unique gift and goodness. If one reads the book slowly enough to assimilate it on a deep level, one enters the presence of magic, which I would equate to the shamanic state of consciousness. Within this numinous realm, one experiences a larger encompassing reality, where revelations, transformation, and healing are possible.

~Malcolm Groome, Shamanic Practitioner

All I can say is . . . stunning, elegant, beautiful. *Love's Cauldron* is moving and compelling -- it's raw and intense in exposing all angles of who the author is and who she's come to be. The trajectory of the book is solid. The prose is beautiful, and the poems possess a rhythm and lyricism that complement their depth. The book is a valuable reflection on life.
~Catherine Parnell, Writer, Editor, Publicist and Educator

❋

I loved this book, as a witness and as a witch. It tells the story many of us never get to tell. One of opening our "psychic eyes" and allowing our intuition to grow us into the "changer of outcomes" instead of full of fear. There has never been a moment where we didn't need women who are not afraid of facing the unknown or realms we cannot see. This is the murmuration and Jennifer has listened deeply.
~Erika Harlow, Mother, Artist, Witch

❋

Jennifer Lehr, artist and healer, shows us the path of an individual with a strong and independent spirit. Her stories and poetry evoke rich visuals and open ancient paths to be tread upon in new ways. The path moves inward as Lehr finds her true voice and purpose. It was an inspiration to read.
~Wanda Chudzinski, Artist

❋

Over the years, I have always taken it as a compliment when people have told me I am in touch with my feminine side. When I think about the timing of those observations, it is usually when I am in the midst of a creative project, playing with my kids & grandkids, enjoying live music or theatre, or having deep philosophical discussions about psychology, spirituality, or human growth. Reading Love's Cauldron made me more conscious and appreciative of my feminine side.
~Mike Bosworth, Author/Speaker/Sales Philosopher

※

Jennifer Lehr has written a fascinating, challenging, and hopeful book. Exploring the human condition, with all its ups and downs, the stories lead the reader in pursuit of self-knowledge, seeking to understand why and how to respond to what comes one's way while traversing the panoply of human experience. Such a variety of events and relationships spill forth that all humanity must find at least some portion of the book with which to relate. An informative and engaging retrospective.
~Carma Floyd, ND

※

A candid, poignant life introspective on the divine feminine's gift of intuitive knowing. A journey of growth and allowance for the inner witch to be called upon to use love and profound inner wisdom as the ultimate healing balm. This revealing, heartfelt tale offers freeing permission for the reader to embrace and reclaim their own knowingness.
~Orcas Island fellow sister of the healing/mystic arts

Author's Notes

Love's Cauldron is both a non-fiction narrative and a memoir. The stories in this book reflect the author's recollection of events. Others may find they remember these events differently. That is okay. Experience is subjective. This book has its own story to tell.

※

Some names, locations, and identifying characteristics have been changed to protect the privacy of those depicted. Dialogue has been re-created from memory.

※

This book is non-linear. Each chapter could be read as a stand-alone essay. Throughout, there is a flow and an untraditional story arc. Imagine the book as a journey through a collage or piece of art.

"When I was younger, I did not know I was a witch. I just knew I was excruciatingly sensitive – seemingly to my detriment. It was only when life forced me to deal with my brokenness that I started on the journey to healing myself and began to be able to manifest my potential. We don't always take this journey. Sometimes we get caught in the mirage that only the external is real and is exclusively where our focus needs to be. We may lose sight of the value of inner exploration and so settle for a much smaller world and much more limited possibilities for ourselves."

~Jennifer J Lehr, LMFT - Love's Cauldron, Book 1 Deliverance

Love's Cauldron

Reclaim Your Wild Feminine

Book 1 Deliverance
The Freeing of Oneself

Jennifer J Lehr, LMFT

Published by Filament Publishing, Ltd
14 Croydon Road, Beddington,
Croydon, Surrey, CR0 4PA
www.filamentpublishing.com

Love's Cauldon by Jennifer Lehr
ISBN 978-1-915465-92-4

© Jennifer J Lehr, 2025
The right of Jennifer J Lehr, to be identified as the author of this work has been asserted by her in accordance with the Copyright, Designs and Patents Act 1988.

All rights reserved.
The book may not be copied in any form without the prior written permission of the publisher.

Cover art: Jennifer Lehr
Cover design: Jennifer Lehr
Book Design by Filament
Printed in the UK and the USA by
Ingram Content Group

Dedicated to the
divine feminine
&
wild witch
in all of us.

Table of Contents

	Preface	11
	Introduction	19
1	My Secret	36
2	Before I Knew Who I Was	62
3	Descent	83
4	Bringing Myself Back	99
5	Releasing The Binds	134
6	The Call To Heal Others	174
7	Weaving Together	210
8	Honoring Spirit	220
9	Love Is The Root	268
10	Our Living Journey	302
	Epilogue	334
	Acknowledgements	337
	About the Author	339

Preface

The Art of Becoming

This is the magic.
This is the power.
This is the root.
This is the key and the gold.
This is the journey.
This is the fairy dust
sprinkled across the land.

This is all of it.

Who I Am

I am a marriage and family therapist, trained and licensed. I have years of practice, supervision, and training. I have trained in Gestalt Theory and therapy, Intersubjectivity, and Emotionally Focused Therapy for Couples. I have training in hypnosis and dreamwork. I have facilitated art therapy groups and co-facilitated a domestic violence group. I have worked with children, teenagers, adults, couples, and families. I am a writer, author, and the creator of a relationship growth app. I host a podcast. I am also a witch. I have talent, capability, depth, and insight. I continue to grow and become. My becoming helps others to become, to unfold into their fuller selves. But in calling myself a witch, I know there will be judgment against me. I know I am stepping into deep, dark waters.

My mother used to say, "Sticks and stones will break your bones, but names will never harm you." As a child, I knew she was wrong. The names flung at me, like flaming balls of animosity, hurt. Still, part of standing in my I AM is showing myself. I am bigger than a role or a box. We all are. And stepping out of our boxes into all of ourselves is part of our healing, part of our destiny, part of the art of becoming.

✴

CONJURE

To summon by a sacred name.
To invoke by incantation or enchantment.
To bring into existence as if by magic.

Scattered. Pieces.
Feelings, chapters, moments.
Each piece a bead.
Unlinked.

A wild wind enters.
The breath of soul,
focus, intention, love.

My arms reach outward, wide.
The pieces gather, coalesce,
pull together.

A pattern emerges. The beads string.
Translucent, greens and golds,
reds, oranges, blues, and purples.
Unformed becomes formed.

Sight opens.

It Is Time

It takes a long time to become a person. A whole-ish person. Our lives are elusive and ephemeral, like smoke wafting, moving, twirling, illuminated, and made visible by a shaft of light. Without the light, we cannot see. Without the light, meaning escapes us. We see ourselves as we look back on the marks we've left, the words we've written, the experiences we've had, the wisdom we have accumulated. We look back and see the footprints behind us, revealing the path we have traversed. If you were a tracker, you could see. By following the feelings, the words. The stories. Slowly, it would emerge, an understanding. A seeing. A knowing.

Untangling

As I read pieces I've written from as far back as over twenty-five years ago, I experience who I was and who I am and the connection between the past me and the present me. Many of my concerns are the same. In some places, I've evolved and transcended. In others, I am still unraveling the same knot.

Life is a weave. Yet, within this weave, certain themes prevail. They carry through and emerge again and again, like waves cresting, over and over.

Fear and intuition twisted together, morphed, dark and light. Untangled strand by strand. Until each could be named as a separate being. Oh, there you are, fear. Oh, there you are, intuition. A relief to untangle this knot. Almost invisible, this journey.

Tree of Love

This book is a tree with many leaves and blossoms, each a burst of brightness, of intention. It is the stars shining and shifting in the night sky as the earth turns. Nothing stays the same, and yet there is an essence holding it, infused through it. I hope you find the essence of love in this work nourishing. Love of others, love of myself, love of the spirit world, love of the natural world. Sometimes, a book writes itself in pieces. Over years. But other parts of life keep it from coming together, keep it from being a focus. I started writing this book many times. And now I begin again, including older bits and pieces. Past, present, and future mix and become a tapestry. Who I am and what I have experienced have a continuity. Older memories interweave with happenings from yesterday. My childhood shows up in my today. My future leads me from who I am now to who I will become tomorrow.

Isn't that how life is? The many and varied moments of a day, of a season, of a decade, of a lifetime. Yet somehow, one's consciousness is strung together through all of these moments, all of these experiences and awarenesses.

Somehow, our lives feel whole despite distinct chapters, each with moments of grief, of the mundane, of beauty, of boredom, and of liveliness.

I look at the patchwork of my life and am amazed. Oh, I was that person, and then I was that person, and then yet another person. But I am still me. And because I am me, because I have lived through many chapters, because I have had many lives within this one, I can know you. I can recognize myself in you. And I hope you can recognize yourself in me.

This is how this book began. In pieces. Little meandering thoughts. Some pieces have been previously published, mostly on my blog. Other bits were stashed away in various folders on my computer or printed and found in old dusty three-ring binders. They've been dug out, read, considered, worked on, and placed.

For those of you who have always wanted to write. Don't be afraid. It is not too late. Find a tiny bit of space and just begin. Perhaps someday, someone will say to you, "It is time. Your soul is hungry."

Acknowledge it.

Love it.

Feed it.

Bless it.

Share it.

Honoring Our Magic

This book is for those of us who wish to grow and heal, who wish to understand the journey and art of becoming. It is for those of us who wish to claim our wild feminine, to unbox ourselves, to free what has been pushed down and locked away. It is for those of us who wish to understand transformation, pull it into our lives, to step more firmly on our journeys. This book is about finding the magic within us and using it to create a new life and new world.

You do not have to be obedient. You are intrinsically worthy. You are leaving your shame behind. You are co-creators with the good. You are the white (not the color of skin but the lightness of being) witches for the good. This book is not about black magic, the twisting and destroying of truth and that which is virtuous. This book is of the good and to be used for the good of all.

This book is for all those who wish to honor the parts of us that are not logical, that are open to magic and intuition.

Magic is the unexpected happenings that come from deeper layers of reality. Intuition is the ability to be in connection with, to have a knowing of these deeper layers beyond our surface lives. Magic includes not only knowledge of these layers but the ability to channel power or information from other dimensions, from deities, guides, spirits, or even ancestors.

This book is for those who know, hear, or see images and information. It is for those of us who want to access the most goodness and wisdom that is available.

Goodness and wisdom are available to us if we tune into them, if we aspire to reach them, to embody them. Goodness is enabled by wisdom, for without wisdom, we would not recognize the value of goodness. Because of the human ego and its unevolved aspects, this is also where black magic comes from – using these talents for the negative, for harm instead of good, out of greed or resentment instead of generosity or love.

This book is for those of us who, regardless of gender, align with the historically suppressed and more feminine qualities of intuition, receptivity, and healing – whether or not you align with the culturally sanctioned and more masculine qualities of structure, logic, and action. It is for those who see intuition as valuable as thinking and receptivity as valuable as taking action. It is for those who honor the rhythms of nature and the body rather than attempt to conquer them. It is for those who embrace the understanding that receiving information and guidance is a valuable talent and gift.

✴

Introduction

The path I am speaking of is not a trail that cuts through canyons and meadow or crisscrosses the mountain. The path I am referring to is the Big Path, the Tao, the Way. It is a path that opens the lungs, fires the spirit, and awakens faith. It is the path of pilgrimage, one that leads straight to the heart of being.
- Tias Little

Little Girl

My connection with my intuitive self, and my understanding of my goodness, and trust in myself shut down early. The happenings in my environment and how I was perceived deeply impacted me.

I am a little girl. My parents are fighting. I see big blocks of hate flying. Sharp, heavy blocks that hit and hurt. My father is bigger than my mother. Scary. I am scared. I hurt. I do not understand why they fight. Why they hurt each other. I retract into myself.

My mother makes trays of cookies for a party.

I take a tray and spill it into the playpen where my brother and sister, twins are, so they can have cookies. They smile and eat cookies. I spill in another tray. I am generous. I want them to be happy. Crumbs and crushed cookies everywhere.

My mother discovers what I have done. She does not see my generosity, my desire to share. She is furious. Yells, hits. I retract further into myself. Further away from people.

I become small and smaller. I become nothing. I begin to hide in the cracks, hide who I am, separate from myself. My parents do not see me. My good intentions, my kind heart. I no longer see myself. I do not know who I am.

Who Are You?

So often, much of ourselves gets lost as we journey through our childhoods into our adult lives. When we are not seen through the eyes of the heart, when others see the worst rather than the best in us or categorize who we are in untrue ways, we may contract and pull into ourselves. We are taught to think about ourselves in pre-determined roles. When we are asked what we want to be when we grow up, we say things like, I want to be a doctor, or a police officer, or an artist. Many of us are not taught that we are growing evolving beings, that our feelings, impulses, and intuitions are important. That the world is bigger than what is obvious.

How many of us are taught that as we walk through the fields of life, there is much to notice, to enjoy? That the earth is beautiful and deserves our love and care.

How important it is to observe, to see, to taste, like the sun-warmed strawberry that bursts its juicy essence into the mouth? That we are part of this, the beauty and spirit of earth?

Most of us are not taught that the trees, water, and sky have spirits, that the planets are beings, that the entire universe is alive. We are not taught that everything is consciousness, that we are part of that consciousness. We are not taught that we can develop the ability to connect with more than our physical and human realm.

Expansion

We are also not taught that a living universe interacts with us, that it may demand the development of ourselves, and that this self-development may have specific steps or phases. These steps and phases vary according to an individual's maturity and many other factors. For me, these steps unfolded, lapping and overlapping, moving forward and then returning to be learned at a deeper level. Rather than discrete steps, they were patterned, a mandala, an expansion from the center. These developmental phases are reflected in the chapters of this book. They reveal my journey of becoming and my ultimate embracing of my witch self.

Whole Conscious Witch

Being a good witch is not just a set of skills such as the ability to hear our inner voice, channel, contact other dimensions, hear our guides, and so on. It is also who we are. A person who wants to bring wisdom and love to the planet.

A person who wants to be aware of the magic of the universe. A person who cares. A person who develops her skills. Develops her heart. Develops her wisdom. And steps into her magic and uses it well. Being a witch is meaningless if we use our power to harm or make living more difficult, for life is already filled with challenges and struggles, accidents, and traumas. It is in the soothing of these difficulties, in metabolizing and transmuting them, that clarity emerges, that we find our healing, and for some of us, our power.

Receptivity

I've known for years that when we create, we often are channeling. When we create, whether through what we ordinarily consider as creative, such as painting or writing, or whether our creating involves healing, transforming consciousness, or some aspect of our lives, to create means we are using our imaginations and openness to inspiration (the in-breath of spirit) to bring something new into awareness or being. When we channel, we are contacting higher dimensions, accessing a new perspective or new information. Of course, we must be receptive and have the structure and knowledge, training, or education in place to allow that particular information to come through. But many of us have access to "guidance," even if we don't call it that. Sometimes, we just know. Sometimes, an event occurs synchronistically that sends us in a particular direction. This is another form of guidance.

Guidance

The difference in being a conscious witch or not is acknowledging that we are guided. And that we use this guidance to heal, to bring in more love, to enlighten our lives and world.

That there is more occurring than the realm of the mind and ego. Our minds and egos are limited. They operate according to what we believe, what we have experienced, what we have been taught. Our ego selves believe that we are singular and do not have a true knowing of the multiplicity we are embedded in and part of. Our egos do not know that we are also the life-filled waters of the ocean and the beaming light of the stars. Listening to our guides allows a larger perspective that lies beyond our personal experience. A perspective that may be like a brisk breeze, rustling, rearranging, and reinforming the contents of our mind, opening and allowing new information and new vistas.

I AM

We are all of us, I AM.

I AM all of us. One and everyone.

I AM the trees and the clouds
The mouse and the eagle
The water and the drought.

I AM the dewdrop glassy clear.

I AM the mourner of the dead,
the greeter of the dawn,
the shifter in the shadows.

I AM the crazed
yelling in the streets,
the forgotten
locked up,
the one
who walked away.

I AM the poor
and the wealthy,
the orphan
and the familied,
the broken
and the whole.

I AM the savior and the saved.
I AM the trapped and the delivered.
I AM the student and the teacher.

I AM the one who is abused.
The one who is addicted.
I AM the one who is abducted, raped, ruined.
I AM the one who suffers, who cries, who
struggles. I AM the one who is cast out,
imprisoned.

I AM the one who turned away
from my inner self,
from my wild woman self
in order to survive.

I AM the one broken who is now becoming whole.
I AM the one returning.
I AM the good, and I AM the light.
Living, loving
myself, all of me.

I AM

I AM

A magician, a witch, a changer of outcomes. This is who I became after I didn't know who I was. Each step was a teacher. With each step, I confronted the obstacles in myself. With each step I made myself anew.

I am an energy shifter. I can change what is and what will be. But here is also where I can get caught. Sometimes, I hold onto my intention and forget to allow the universe to do its part. I must remember, take the action, let go of the results. I am a creator, but I am not in control of everything. I can shift energy, but others have their own paths, their own destinies, and must make their own decisions.

I breathe in and reorganize myself, my world, with words, actions, feelings, thoughts. I breathe out into the world and allow the stardust to disperse. I do not know where the golden flecks will settle, what will change. I do not know who will make use of my offerings. I breathe in, and I breathe out.

Each of us is an energy shifter. We may not know it. We may have been defeated. We may be caught in an entrapment or a situation such as poverty... and so do not activate this part of ourselves. Not in this story or this life. But there will come a time. For we exist through eons, returning again and again to develop, to experience, to learn, grow, and give.

Each of us will find our magic. And if our hearts are open, we will spread our magic across the universe.

Our Stories

The witches I grew up with included those in The *Wizard of Oz*. They were witches from other realms and had magical powers. I loved Glinda the Good Witch. I hated and feared the Wicked Witch of the West. Yet they were witches that grew out of stereotypical ideas. They were witches who were not seen in their full power but caught in the net of human projection, whom others had dumped their debris on. Consequently, they were fragmented caricatures, all good or all bad, and given qualities such as repulsive hag, beautiful sorceress, or cunning trickster. Those witches appeared and disappeared, seemingly at whim, static beings without future or history. I never considered how they had become who they were (and the limitations they were reduced to) because *The Wizard of Oz* wasn't their story. It wasn't the story of the witch. It was Dorothy's story.

But this book is about our story. Each of us has a story. A story that reveals a rich and complex human being. Each of us started somewhere and is on the journey to becoming. Some of us are becoming witches or just discovering that we are witches. Others are already fully aligned with being a witch.

This is my story of opening and cooperating with other realms. This is my story of healing and opening to love. This is my story of becoming a good witch.

The Word Witch

I have struggled with the word witch. I have struggled because the word witch is pejorative, because it has been linked to evil, because it comes with judgment and blame, with definitions including, "a woman supposed to have dealings with the devil."

For this reason, I have been more comfortable with the words healer, shaman, or even wizard. Wizard, for example, is linked with the definitions of knowing, philosopher, sage. But it is the word witch that needs to be re-visioned, re-defined, re-recognized to its truer meaning. It is the word witch that needs to be understood as an aspect of what we are, of what we can become, of those who have a skill set that can help heal our world.

Seeing Beyond

Because of our rejection of both the word and the qualities embodied by witch, it is as if we are missing a limb. An essential part of us is not acknowledged, much less celebrated. Consequently, we generally don't think of ourselves as witches, energy shifters, or transformers – people who have a capacity that extends beyond the conventional, people who can see beyond what the five senses reveal, people who can change outcomes, people who can heal. Yet among us are many who have aligned themselves with inner sight, with guidance, with an open heart, and the ability to connect to more than our physical and tangible world. There are herbalists and medicine women who hear the voices of plants, earth mothers who tune into moon cycles, astrologers who can read the mythology of the planets, psychics who see potential realities, writers who bring in voices and stories. These are people who use their wisdom and goodness and their ability to see beyond everyday reality to enlighten our planet and lives, to heal that which has been broken, to guide and offer insight to those who have become lost or are simply on their journey of development.

I think of a woman I know who spends much of her time in prayer, shifting energies, holding harmony so that chaos does not erupt in various outer world situations.

I think of other witch practitioners who also work with the collective, using their abilities to mitigate violence and increase peace in various parts of the world. These groups of people work in specific ways. Others work differently. I, for example, may breathe healing into lost parts of a person or lost parts of myself, helping those rejected or cast-out parts reintegrate into the whole. Releasing those energies so that they may enrich rather than detract from that being. Perhaps some were born with these abilities, and they developed without mishap and easily. That is not my story. I came into this life scared. Life threw many obstacles that took me down to breaking points. It is through those cracks that I began to make the changes that allowed me to become a fuller human and eventually to open to cooperating with what I call "my guides."

This was not intended or expected, but it was and is my path of healing – the ongoing journey of my life.

Past Life Learning

In my process of learning, of becoming, of embracing all of me, I have explored the idea of past lives and even taken trainings to allow me to develop the ability to see deeper into energy patterns, happenings, and stories. Whether these stories are actual past lives or metaphors, they inform us and allow us to resolve aspects of our lives that feel stuck. One of the stories that has emerged for me is Mirembe's story.

Mirembe's Story

167 A.D. Mirembe is fifty-seven years old with grown children and grandchildren. She is a village healer in Africa who receives visions. She often guides those who come to her.

A drought came to this land, and the villagers suffered. They lost animals and crops. It was decided that a curse had settled over them. Some of the villagers began to talk about Mirembe. She must be responsible. The village elders came and grabbed her, dragged her out of her home, out of the village, across the dry brush to a parched, dusty patch of earth. She was accused and yelled at, put in a pit, her lower body trapped, her upper body, head, and face exposed. She was surrounded by a group of villagers, hate in their eyes. Accusation in their throats. Closed hearts.

People she had helped turned against her. They had already gathered the pile of stones. Mirembe begged to be released, told them she only wanted good for the village.

They did not listen. The first man picked up a stone and threw it. It hit her in the head. Dazed, she would have fallen, but for the pit she was trapped in. Another stone struck her. She screamed as her heart broke. She screamed in pain. And then another stone, and another. Blood, shattered bones, the side of her face crushed. It took a long time before she fell unconscious. They stoned her until she was dead. Her body broken; her head cracked open. Her blood black on the earth. They left her there. Later, her children gathered and did ceremony over her dead body. They whispered words of love and released her spirit to the afterlife.

As Mirembe suffered and died, she decided that people could not be trusted. She decided that this horrible thing that happened to her meant she was nobody, meant she was unworthy, that she did not have true spiritual power. She decided that she would no longer show herself. People were not safe. The world was not safe.

✷

Mirembe, I feel your voice inside of me, the voice of the betrayed, the voice of the broken, the voice of those who were destroyed and thrown away. I hear your voice, your words, "You are nobody. Who are you to claim your powers, to write this book? Who are you to show yourself, to believe in yourself?" The voice of self-hate. The voice that takes blame for what has been done to us, to witches.

But we are not to blame. We are not unworthy. We are the witches of the world. We are reclaiming who we are.

It is time to take back our rightful place as holders of magic, as healers, as those who help smooth the troubles of this world. It is time to claim our value, to know who we are and what we offer. It is time to enrich and enliven what it is to be human with the fullness of who we are.

Mirembe, you are inside of me, one of my many lives, one of my lives where my soul experienced murder for who I was. Your life is entwined with mine. I am here now, in a new life, in a life that is different. I am safe. We are safe in this life.

Mirembe, this world is one that has buried our witches and humanity's power with them. Our witches have been chased off, tortured, burned, stoned, and then they and we have run from ourselves, from our magic, from our knowing. Our world is lost without our witches. It is lost without the divine feminine, the secrets of the dark side of the moon, the realm of feelings and body. Our world is lost without intuition and magic.

Mirembe, let go of that death, that pain, that betrayal. You are worthy. It is time to claim who you are, to release the past. You are within me, and this wound is mine to heal. Mirembe, I am credentialed, trained. I have the education, skill, intuition, access to guidance, and the deep seeing of a witch. I have the right to show who I am. I have the right to stand tall.

May my healing, your healing help all of us who were wronged in this way to find our power and strength, our wholeness. We are not hiding anymore. We are removing the veil. We are stepping forward into our full worth.

Mirembe, remember, we are, I AM Witch.

Righting

Another purpose of this book is to take a stand, to right what has been maligned for centuries. To make being a witch simply an expansion of who we already are or of what we have the potential to become. To redefine what a witch is. To see a witch as an energy shifter who is deeply attuned to subtle layers of reality – as someone who can use their talents to spread magic through healing and love.

Historically, witches have been punished, blamed for what we do not understand. When the baby dies or the crop fails, in our small, disconnected selves, in our inability to tolerate the largeness and mystery of the universe, it must be someone else's fault. This fault has been cast upon those who are not understood. Often on witches. They have been demonized in fairy tales and real life. They have been drowned, tortured, and burned to death. To fully understand the impact of what has been done to those named witches, this short description of death by burning will elucidate the pain and horror that witches have been subjected to.

Death by Burning
In the process of being burned to death, a body experiences burns to exposed tissue, changes in content and distribution of body fluid, fixation of tissue, and shrinkage (especially of the skin). Internal organs may be shrunken due to fluid loss. Shrinkage and contraction of the muscles may cause joints to flex and the body to adopt the "pugilistic stance" (boxer stance), with the elbows and knees flexed and the fists clenched. Shrinkage of the skin around the neck may be severe enough to strangle a victim. Fluid shifts, especially in the skull and in the hollow organs of the abdomen, can cause pseudo-hemorrhages in the form of heat hematomas. The organic matter of the body may be consumed as fuel by a fire. The cause of death is frequently determined by the respiratory tract, where edema or bleeding of mucous membranes and patchy or vesicular detachment of the mucosa may be indicative of inhalation of hot gases. Complete cremation is only achieved under extreme circumstances.

The amount of pain experienced is greatest at the beginning of the burning process before the flame burns the nerves, after which the skin does not hurt. Many victims die quickly from suffocation as hot gases damage the respiratory tract. Those who survive the burning frequently die within days as the lungs' alveoli fill with fluid and the victim dies of pulmonary edema.
~Wikipedia

This and other "punishments" enacted on those not understood (who were overwhelmingly female and often part of a marginalized group) show utter ignorance and desire to harm.

Even today, in 2025, in various areas of the world, including Africa, Southeast Asia, and Latin America, women are still accused of being witches and may be sent off to a "witch camp," beaten to death, lynched, or some other equally horrible violation. The beliefs out of which these punishments emerge reveal the malevolent side of humanity where we destroy those whom we find threatening instead of looking at each person as a source of abundance, someone whose contributions could enrich our lives, our culture, our planet. It is akin to taking a beautiful and amazing being and smashing her to smithereens.

✶

Free

Who wants each person to be the same?
To fit in a box. Divorced from their inner power?

How do we break free?

The wave is big. Too big to control.
We step forward into our power in multitudes.
Sheets of light, crystalline structures. Indra's net.
The sparkle spreads through each of us.
A murmuration, a shimmering radiance.
Like sunlight dancing on water.

We are flying.

1
My Secret

And the day came when the risk to remain tight in a bud was more painful than the risk it took to blossom.

✳

Opening
I have a secret, a part of my life I do not share with most people. I have a fear of sharing this part, although that is changing, and I am opening. Hiding no longer serves the person I have become.

Childhood
As a child, I was cautious about being open with my parents. I didn't want to be yelled at or punished. They weren't always safe. My father's temper caused him to hit us or sometimes break a chair in his anger. He could be mean and taunt us. I remember him calling me ugly.

My mother also, at times, had moments of rage and unpredictable behavior. When I was three and learning to swim, she pushed me into the pool when I wasn't looking because she couldn't tolerate my fear or hesitation. She had no understanding of trust.

We hide when we are afraid. Afraid of being judged. Afraid of being hurt. Afraid of being outcast. Afraid of not being good enough. Because we know it is not safe to show ourselves or share our beliefs.

The emotional atmosphere of my family, critical rather than supportive, and the occasional violent outbursts left me cautious.

My Secret

I am a witch. This is my secret. I believe in spiritual guides, master guides, archangels. I believe in other dimensions. I believe in my inner voice. I know the voice of intuition can be developed, that it is a doorway to even greater knowing. I have kept this secret because witches have been persecuted for their knowing. But this knowing is part of my power, and it is time for it to be shared.

I listen when I experience a strong feeling or when my solar plexus heats up, or I hear a voice that says, "Yes, do that." I communicate with my guides daily. I ask questions; I listen for answers. I use a pendulum. Working with a pendulum means I have an object, usually a crystal, on the end of a chain. I hold the chain and let the crystal dangle.

The pendulum is sensitive to electromagnetic energy. (This is similar to dowsing to find water.) Our guides can influence this energy and cause the pendulum to move. For me, a yes answer occurs when the pendulum moves counterclockwise. When it swings toward and away from me, the answer is a no. With practice, as we learn to "listen," we may also hear words, sentences or see images.

I occasionally have readings with psychics and astrologers. I have worked weekly with a woman who is clairvoyant, who helps me find where I get stuck so I can un-mire myself and connect with a higher vision. I believe that help is available to us in many ways: inspiration, teachings, and spiritual support.

Seeking

What is the way? How do we find it? I know that in the chaos of my earlier life, I was desperate for guidance. Somebody, please tell me what to do, how to be. Help me get rid of my fear and confusion, my sense of pain, and being overwhelmed. This, in a sense, was an underworld. A world of fear and anxiety. The dim counterpart to feeling secure, trusting, worthy, and confident.

My insecurity, my sense of fear, my not knowing my worth caused me to seek. First, I sought approval, an acknowledgment that I was special, of value, worthy, good enough. I outgrew that. Later, I sought philosophies, spiritual traditions, knowledge, healing. I was on a path of seeking. I wanted to step out of my fear and step into knowing. I wanted to feel sure of myself, of my decisions. I wanted to know I was okay, that I had value. I wanted to find safety in an unsafe world. This desire led me to all kinds of exploration.

I was looking for guidance. I was looking for an inner knowing and clarity about who I was and an understanding of my purpose.

When I was younger, I attached to an outer, external, tangible goal. I will be this or do that. I worked toward that goal. My focus helped me push through my inner chaos. At the same time, I studied and learned methods of divination like the tarot, astrology, and I Ching.

I read about past lives and reincarnation. Later, my therapeutic and mindfulness work opened even more channels of inner hearing.

These skills and methods enabled me to deepen my self-understanding, gain more control over my inner chaos, and heal. I came to understand that we carry patterns from previous lifetimes, including patterns that need to be unwound and released. I learned to listen with my body. See images, stories. Hear words, sentences. Receive guidance.

Whether using a pendulum, feeling into my body, or divining with the tarot, I ask for spiritual wisdom and guidance. I ask my guides, "May you show me whatever is in the highest good for all." I open myself up to seeing more than I can see with my eyes. I ask that I see the best and most positive path for the situation. I don't see divination as predictive because we deal with possibilities and probabilities. While we live within big astrological cycles, we have the power of choice, even if only in our attitudes; in this sense, little is set in stone or static.

Star Life

Pulsating Star
Alcyone - Blue Giant
Arcturus
Sirius
Betelgeuse.

Birthing, dying
double and binary.
Dwarf and Giant.
Red, blue, yellow.

Constellations of stars
Big Dipper
Ursa Minor
Virgo and Pegasus.

Populating the night sky.
Worlds away.

Living Universe

The universe is so much bigger than the human mind can hold. Awareness resides everywhere, within every object, manifest and unmanifest. The planets and galaxies are beings with consciousness. Cards, sticks, coins, and birthtimes can reveal perspectives, guidance, and knowledge to the intuitive. This way of seeing uses means beyond our five ordinary senses. Like a radio that can pick up frequencies and translate them into sound, we, too, can pick up frequencies and translate them.

For me, being guided means living in a universe, extensive and populated with more than humans, inhabited by others with more wisdom and greater perspective. It is my way of reaching out and touching what I could not reach in other ways. It is my way of feeling safe. I've kept this part of myself secret. I haven't shared my beliefs or the reach of my sight. I've held this close to myself, protected and away from the judgment of others.

I Am a Witch

I didn't start as a witch. I developed into a witch.

I look like a normal person. But because I have capacities that not everyone has developed, capacities that are still viewed as suspect, I am afraid of being judged. I hide. I am afraid of words that cut, thoughts that harm. I am afraid of being called crazy, of being misunderstood. Of being diminished. I am afraid of saying, yes, I listen to my guides, my inner voice first. That doesn't mean I'm crazy. It means I see more, have access to more.

Despite our skills, we bleed like everyone else. We drown. Our fragile bodies can be hurt, damaged. We give birth. We nurture. We care. We feel. Witches, women.

A human body and a human life. Still, it is easy to turn the evil eye. Judgment. And so, those of us who are not understood have hidden.

Who gets judged? Many of us. Not just witches. Everyone different is suspect. Our world caught in divisions. When will we see past the differences? When will we embrace instead of separate?

Magic Enters

Magic, the art of influencing events
using hidden natural forces,
cooperating with spiritual beings.

I breathe life into this form.
The closed circle opens and becomes a spiral.
Round and round begins to move upward.
Beings enter. The dove. The seer. The sight.

I put down the heavy load I carry.
I breathe in.
A translucent mist fills my cells.
I feel myself loosen. Open.
Possibilities expand.

I allow myself to believe.
I allow myself to be influenced.
Guided.

Magic enters.

Soul Weary

In 2020, my business was struggling. I was bogged down with work. I was tired, soul weary. I felt like I was standing before a big open space. I could not see what was next but knew change was approaching. How do I navigate through these challenges? How do I best see?

I knew I needed guidance. I needed the winds of someone with a stronger vision and more sight to blow through me and whip the cobwebs away.

Soul's Desire

I arranged a session with a new clairvoyant. Someone my sister had used. Sylvia. Images came to her. As she spoke, I felt her images enter me, infusing me with hope and new life. The drudgery of surviving a brutal winter became the new green promise of spring.

She told me my soul needed to write this book. I knew she was right. I had just spent ten years on a project and could see that much of what I had created needed to be revamped and reorganized. I looked at how I focused, pushed, and drove myself on this project and how the result was more work. And now I needed to find the time to write.

So, while I had a mountain of work ahead of me, I knew I had to relax my grasp. I had to loosen my hold. I had to find a way not only to reorganize that project but also to grab onto what my soul wanted.

I had to stop trading the present for the future, not only by releasing how tightly I held myself to my task but also by allowing the voice of my soul to sing and reveal its secrets.

Because I would be piecing together writing done over years and new writing, Sylvia told me to use the image of a Japanese cherry tree for this book. Even now, as I write this, I can see it. Covered with pink blossoms. Bees buzzing, gathering pollen, Butterflies sipping nectar. Each blossom has its own bit of life, its own story, its own unique beauty, but is part of the entirety of the tree.

Sylvia's words moved through me. Good news and success coming. One angel on each side of me, holding my hands. I was not alone, and I would not be dropped. I had to open myself and allow change to move in. Trust. Stop the grinding working.

The Silver Dove

I had been trying to develop trust for years. That word. That quality. But how to embody it? How to make it alive inside? How to live in the place of trust?

Sylvia saw a silver dove. Saw her bringing ideas and insight to me as I worked. Would I communicate with the Silver Dove? Ask her to show up? Be consciously receptive to her?

"You need peace," Sylvia said, "a break. Your soul is hungry to be fed. Stop the thinking, stop the "what to do, what to do" mantra. Let go for a while. Write a letter to god. What do you want? Put it in a drawer. Let the angels do their work."

What makes me happy? Writing for passion. Asking god and the Silver Dove to be with me, making the time to write. I will. I do.

I begin to piece together, as if making a quilt out of cloth shapes, each with its own color, pattern, and texture, something whole.

Coalesce

I was not born with an extraordinary gift. I was born with extreme sensitivity, which is both a gift and a curse. I can reach out and imagine. I have learned to find the story and have it emerge, coalesce, settle down in front of me. As a therapist, I have sat with clients and seen and felt their stories as they began to speak. I see where their work is, where they are not yet grounded or have not yet opened their wings. I see where they are stuck and need help adjusting, shifting, rearranging who they are. This is a talent for which I am grateful.

This gift, my sensitivity, is not actually a curse. It is simply a place that needs love, attention so that I may grow what I need to be whole. I have had trouble staying in my own experience when I am with others. I step into your body, feel what is yours instead of what is mine. Your pain, your struggle. I have given myself away over and over because I was not here. Instead of tending me, I was in you.

Rooting

But I am growing roots. Deep down into the earth. I am becoming rooted. Without these roots, I cannot find my own life, my own presence, my own self.

Growing roots is a process that involves pain. To grow roots, I've had to dig deep into my failures. I've had to see my weaknesses. I had to understand why I gave too much away, why I needed what I needed. I've had to examine and reconstruct myself.

Until I began growing roots, I could not grow wings. Once rooted, my self-work changed. Once rooted, I was free to grow wings. Unlike my earlier years, I was safe enough in my own soil to trust my perceptions. Safe enough to open my intuition more completely. I began to inhabit my life more fully while also connecting to images, thoughts, ideas, and support that was more ethereal and not from the human realm.

Magical Being

The Silver Dove puts thoughts in my head. She is beautiful, with soft silvery feathers. She weaves feminine intuition, inner and spiritual knowledge from the ethereal into physical reality.

Her silver colors speak of a feminine witchy energy and the moon. I see her flying, a sparkling thread in her mouth as she weaves and stitches spirit with form. As she brings thoughts into my mind.

Because she can fly, because she is ethereal, she has perspective and can see more than I can see.

I see up to the next hill, but she sees what is beyond. She sees what I need to convey my thoughts. When I am writing, I can feel her enter. I feel the quality of my writing change. She sends messages and assists me.

She is my friend and guide. She makes me more than a physical being, but a being infused with magic, magical thoughts, and sight.

Winged Heart

We all have the potential to both fully inhabit ourselves and to fly.

Fully inhabiting ourselves means that we feel our feelings. It means we live on this earth and recognize ourselves as part of it. Our earth is our keeper, and we are her keeper. It means we see ourselves as a part of her biology, part of her spirit.

Flying means our imagination and intuition are open. It means we know we are more than our biology. It means we know more is available to us than the doorways of the five senses. It means we are not afraid of what we do not know. We are not afraid of the feminine qualities of intuition, of knowing, of being guided or interacting with other dimensions.

The link between these two places, our imagination, and our intuition, is our open heart. Our open heart allows us to love. To love ourselves and other earthly beings. Our heart connects to the entire universe and those who are part of us, who we are part of, those we often cannot see but can feel and so know and trust are there.

❋

Fear

You persecute
what you do not understand.
The twisting black snake
hanging on the dead branch
frightens you.

You miss
the seeing eyes.
The sensing forked tongue,
the smooth textured sheath
that wraps
and moves with stealth.

The shedding of skin
means growth.
Expansion.
Rebirth.
More life.

This snake means no harm.
Has no evil intentions.

This snake
not a harbinger of evil
or a messenger of magic
or anything but
what it is.

This snake
just a creature of the world.
Living, celebrating
it's one life
as it can.

Soul Memory Discovery

In 2007, I took a class called Soul Memory Discovery with master teacher Ellen Kaufman Dosick. As you might imagine, this class was esoteric. It dealt with hearing our guides, contacting other realms, and healing by working with universal forces to shift energy. (Soul Memory Discovery is a healing modality that helps us access, identify, and relate to issues that limit our lives and keep us from full expression of our Essence and Being.) In this class, we learned how to work with the pendulum. We learned to hear our guides. We each received a Soul Memory Discovery three-ring binder with an energy balance, an invocation, a number of channeled processes designed to shift energies and heal, and a closing process.

I had been seeing Ellen for the past several years for readings. I first saw her in probably 2004 for a reading and saw her yearly thereafter. I've always loved readings. Astrology, psychic, tarot. I remember my first reading in North Philadelphia in the early 80s. Barbara. She told me the name of the person I would soon be dating. The man with whom I would begin my first relationship.

Ellen wore colorful, flowing, draping garments. A skilled social worker who was a therapist for years helping others, she is grounded in both science and spiritual tradition. During readings, we sat across from each other in her office, which was filled with books, thoughts, energies, gemstones, and crystals.

In my first session with her, she talked to me about what I wanted to learn or change. She asked me questions.

What was happening in my life? I was struggling in my first marriage and talked to her about my difficulties. Then we drank water to hydrate our bodies since we would be working with big energies.

We did a simple energy balance to ground our bodies. Ellen opened her book of processes. She read an invocation and invited in the higher beings of light and healing. As she invited in these beings of light, Archangels, master guides, and more, I felt the energy in the room shift. I felt it enliven. I felt the power in it. I felt more in the room than the two of us. I felt tingly and emotional.

Most of us don't think of the beings who are a part of our lives but exist in other realms. Think of Quan Yin, the goddess of compassion, and of the other gods and deities people pray to: God, Muhammad, Jesus, Allah, Shiva, Buddha, Brahma, and Ganesha, the various saints and Archangels. Each being represents something and holds a specific energy. Jesus holds the energy of love. Quan Yin holds the energy of compassion. Whether these beings are archetypal energy configurations or something else, we have the ability to call them to us and interact with them.

Using her pendulum, Ellen asked the beings who filled the room with light, energy, and power which processes in her Soul Memory Discovery binder I needed. We cleared my energy. I spoke aloud specific words to enable specific energy shifts. Then Ellen received images, and a story emerged, a past life impacting me and my first marriage. A story from long ago of struggle and out-of-balance dynamics between a man and a woman.

The man was a drunk. The woman had many children and worked herself to the bone so the family could survive. In my current life, my husband was making a reparation to me, supporting me while I went to graduate school and completed my internships. But the inner dynamics, his sense of being emasculated by me, and my sense that he was closed off and unavailable echoed strongly. I remember leaving with a sense of understanding that I didn't have before walking into her office. I remember realizing how I was difficult for him and deciding I needed to be softer with him. A trust of my guides was being established.

Accessing Spirit

It is curious to me how many people do not trust this realm of experience. A realm that has become familiar and essential to me. How do people live and guide themselves without active contact with the spiritual realm? And yet, I understand. The grip of both embodied reality and belief systems is strong. We are wired for survival, to noticing what is in our physical world, and to listening to the voices and beliefs of our family and community.

I am not of religious background, but spiritual, claimed through learning and inclination. My father was agnostic but raised Lutheran. My mother was atheist but raised Jewish. I have learned to open myself and see beyond specific religious lenses. I have learned to view from a vantage point that allows all to be honored.

My trust in this realm is integrated into my daily life. I have pendulums in various spots in my home.

I sometimes pick one up and ask a question. I am always open to what I hear because I want a bigger perspective and more expansive wisdom.

This helps me know that there is more than what I see. I can feel truth, beauty, and peace. I call these "higher" qualities because I strive towards them, even as I strive to accept the parts of myself that are "heavier." Sometimes I "know" something. I feel it in my gut. Or a thought enters my mind. This is channeling. We all do this to different degrees. But some people are more tuned in, more conscious of this process, more able to co-operate with other dimensions. They have developed more ability to do so.

Think of the writer, artist, or inventor who gets an idea. Much of this comes from other realms. We are like tuning forks, radio receivers, conduits.

✵

Soul Memory Reclaimed

The Soul Memory Discovery training I took in 2007 was ten days long, split into three sessions. A friend took the training with me. We drove from LA to San Diego and stayed at a retreat center in the California scrub brush and low desert. We were close to the earth, surrounded by the sounds of birds and wildlife by night and by the energy of the students, Ellen, and the spirits during the day.

We worked with invocation and words. We called in our master guides and beings of light. We learned how to use pendulums. We identified our guides and learned to hear what they wished to say to us.

I used the Soul Memory Discovery process of healing with others for a while. It was challenging for me. I could bring in information, mythology, images, and stories that helped explain and resolve current challenges and dilemmas. I could bring in words, thoughts, guidance, but I was left exhausted and with a pounding headache. I had the ability, but it was difficult for me and was not to be my way of working. After a few years of using this process with others, I instead used the processes mostly on myself to gain clarity and, on occasion, with friends or relatives.

The learning I did in the workshop changed my life. I had always struggled with not knowing what choices to make in my life. Growing up, I was led to believe that if I made a bad choice, I would fall off the edge into irreparable darkness and disaster. I often felt paralyzed. Learning to hear guidance helped me. Instead of being in fear, I simply asked what was best for me. I trusted. I didn't always get an answer, but often I did.

Guidance

Sometimes, we must find the answers ourselves through the process of living. There may be an event that gives us clarity or knocks us over, requiring us to look more closely at ourselves or reorganize our lives. This is a kind of guidance. Other times, guidance is available to us when we ask, or we might be guided by a flash of intuition or knowing. When writing, I have, at times, heard specific instructions. *Go to chapter seven, page two, paragraph three, and put the information there.*

I am in contact with my guides daily. I continually have questions about my life, how to navigate through difficult circumstances, what choices to make. I have learned that there is a knowing that is clearer than my own. Developing a relationship with this higher knowing has brought me gifts. I see with more clarity. I am in alignment with my purpose and mission. Fear has diminished. I continue to work on trusting and integrating trust into my body, molecule by molecule.

Superstition

I think of witchcraft and the fear and superstition people had and still have of witches and their abilities, a fear that enables hate to be thrown about, horrors to unfold. And the current unease of recognizing anything beyond what we can hear, taste, touch, smell, and see, unless, of course, it is the words of organized religion, and we are following a well-trod path. The inability to believe in more than what our physical being perceives is paramount to our attachment to the idea that the earth is the center of the universe. When we cannot accept reality, we twist it and make it conform to our wishes.

We cut off the offending organs and limbs that are reaching outside of the box.

But to honor our ability to contact the divine, to make ourselves the authority is scary because it is subjective. Because there is not just one answer. Because an answer for one person could be different for another. Because we want to see the world as right and wrong. Black and white. We don't understand the difference between intuition and fear. We want life to be simple. We want to blame those who scare us. We want to be good and them to be bad. But to live a life of vaster vision and kindness, we must cast judgment aside and trust the universe and our guides.

Inter-Subjectivities

I remember once, a friend and I received guidance about the same event. We were together, but each heard opposing instructions. We were puzzled. So, we talked about what we heard, and something shifted. Our hearts moved to a more open place. We came to an agreement. That was the intention. That was why we heard what we heard.

We reside in a world of inter-subjectivities, each affecting the other. Two stones thrown into the pool of water. The concentric circles moving outward, meeting each other, an interaction occurs. We each have a guidance system, whether we are tuned into it or not. Truth comes from many places: science, physics, mythology. It comes from our imagination and our intuition. And it may come from other realms, other beings.

Your Healing, My Healing

When I was doing Soul Memory Discovery work with others, I had a series of women come for sessions who had stories emerge around persecution for being suspected witches in another life. Often, when we have a series of clients with a similar issue, we are working through this issue in our own lives. I undoubtedly was trying to bring to consciousness and heal my past life traumas around persecution for my intuitive abilities.

One woman I worked with had a past life where she had been locked in her home with her female lover. The kitchen was filled with dried herbs used for healing. Their home was set on fire as a mob stood outside yelling. They died together.

Each of these different women and I explored the images that emerged, the traumas they had experienced. Those wounds were seeping into their present-day realities. I worked with them, found the healing that each required. The terror or self-blame that needed to be released.

Releasing Trauma

Historically, intuitive women, healers, who might also be mothers or wives, young or old, could be called witches. These were often highly perceptive and sensitive women. These were people with something to contribute to humankind. As witches, they could be persecuted. They could be tormented. Thrown into a well and left to die. Locked into a building and burned to death. Witches on trial hearing ugly words. Witches burned at the stake.

The echo of these terrors resides in our DNA; it swirls through the ethers. It asks to be released and healed.

I don't remember all the stories I heard when I used the Soul Memory Discovery process with other women. I do remember how, as a guide, I entered the story with them, felt their experience with them, helping these women navigate through the fear, persecution, pain, the sense of betrayal, and often death that they had incurred. How I would help them make a decision or a shift in perspective so that they could be free of the trauma, so they could un-encumber themselves from that previous horror. I watched the recognition in their eyes as the story that emerged helped them make sense of their current struggle. I watched them shake off the pain, the betrayal, the fear, and step more fully into themselves and their power. Together, we were able to dislodge stuck energy and bring in healing.

Upward Reach, Downward Dig

I don't tell many people about this part of my life. But as I get older and my skills become more refined, I am grateful for this gift. I wonder how others can navigate their lives without the assistance of other realms. Maybe they don't and are on a rocky ride. Maybe they do, but just access their guidance differently than I.

For me, reaching upward to spiritual guidance is intricately connected to digging downward into the pain of the embodied self. To dig downward into my wounds and traumas without support would feel as if I were lost. Whenever I dig downward, I break through to a different place. Something gets integrated.

To reach upward without digging down was what I did when I was younger. I disconnected from my body, from my knowing. I sought transcendent experiences. I thought I could get to that place without feeling the grief and pain that I had locked inside of me. I thought I could get there without bringing my body along.

My Pony

When I was young, and my pet pony, Nickel, was given away without my knowledge, I spiraled downward into depression. I lost the memory of this occurrence for years. I wasn't able to recover it until I was on my own and in a supportive healing environment. When the original event occurred, I pushed it away but was left with a debilitating grey cloud around me. My joy was gone. My trust was gone. Had I attempted to find that joy and trust without acknowledging the trauma, it would have come in the form of an addiction or escape of some kind.

For me, it came as workaholism and chasing after the feeling of love. Because that sad, depressed child was still there, and until she was tended to, joy and trust would be tainted. If we wish to be whole, we cannot avoid the underworld. We cannot avoid our deep feelings. We cannot avoid the human condition and our challenges. They are part of the journey.

Recovering the Disowned

Working as a therapist, I found that some people "got rid" of parts of themselves, usually as children. They didn't have the capacity to keep these parts in their consciousness, and so these disowned parts would create havoc. An addiction that kept reoccurring and nearly destroyed one woman's life, for example. But digging down, she found the deeper feelings about her childhood, her feelings about her father's mistreatment of her mother, her feelings about her mother's dependency. Her acceptance of having been a "bad" child rather than looking at the pain of not being hugged or tended to. As these pieces were uncovered, slowly, for even a light touch was incredibly uncomfortable, her life began to smooth out. She began to like herself more. The unidentified self-hatred went away. This is the process of going deeper. This is the process of finding our freedom by digging into our pain.

Moving down into our pain can be tricky. If we get stuck there, the feeling of powerlessness can be traumatizing. Instead, we develop the ability to "go down" and return and understand it as a valuable skill. We learn that the feelings we encounter are temporary but necessary. We begin to trust ourselves and this process more. We learn to balance the seeking of "god" with tending to the more hurt parts of ourselves.

There are always people who are incredibly intuitive, psychic even, who do not heal their deeper emotional wounds. And those who heal their emotional wounds but do not open to their guidance. There are those who do neither and those who do both. But we find ourselves more completely by developing all of us. By digging into our pain and by accessing our higher selves. This completes an energy circuit (I see a circle of energy moving from under to above, allowing us to be fully plugged in) and enables us to become healed, conscious, and realized witches.

Murmuration

To do both, digging into our pain and accessing our higher selves, becoming a realized witch is not everyone's calling. But it is an invitation to develop more of ourselves.

We all have the ability to develop access to our guidance in some way or another. I run and have run Soul Collage® groups. In these groups, each member creates what is similar to a personal tarot deck using collage. We use those cards to do readings, to find our inner voices, to learn more about our unseen selves. Invariably, most of the members of my groups, while drawn to this process, are hesitant to join because they do not see themselves as creative. But once in the process, they are delighted to learn that they are creative, that they can "read" the cards, that they can see deeper into their own and the other member's psyches.

As we integrate our inner parts and voices with other aspects, some of which are larger than us, we weave a more resilient cloth. We have access to so much. We are so much. We are a murmuration, a grouping, a community.

We have god within us and without us. We are interconnected with other dimensions. We are part of a multidimensionality.

We stand in this knowing. We stand in seeing who we are and what we are capable of. We stand in trust of ourselves, trust in the universe, trust in our guides. We no longer need to hide.

2
Before I Knew Who I Was

Diamonds have a crystalline structure and are one of the hardest naturally occurring substances known. They are formed from carbon deep within the earth, under tremendous pressure and high temperatures. Like diamonds, we are formed by the pressures upon us. We have the capacity to develop strength and become a prism reflecting light from our facets.
~Jennifer J. Lehr, LMFT

※

Trapped

Sitting at the kitchen table, dinner time. A time of torture. A time I wished myself away from. A nightly ritual that goes on for years. I am sitting to my mother's right on the long side of the rectangular table, facing the window. One of my brothers sits next to me. My father, at the other end, across from my mother. Then, my other brother and sister across the table. Mom, me, Ethan, Dad, Adam, Eva.

My father is sometimes fun, silly. Today, he reaches across and whacks one of my siblings across the head. I cringe. I can feel it. Their pain, humiliation, embarrassment. Shame. Spreads. Into me.

Mean. I want to yell. To stop it. I have fantasies of picking up the big kitchen knife and making my father stop, making him be different.

My mother insists we all eat together at dinner. She feels it is important. That it makes us a family. We are a family, broken together.

I have no power. No ability to change what is. And I do not know who I am.

Embodied Journey

Born through the body of our mothers, we enter this world bloodied and ready to start our embodied journey. We come in with personality traits, quirks, preferences. Like a baby sea turtle newly hatched and pointed to the ocean, we may have a knowing of our direction, of who we are, of who we are to become, a pull towards something. Or we may sense it only vaguely, the direction of our development elusive. Who am I? Who am I supposed to be? How do I want to engage with this life? What is my purpose?

This sense may be fragmented, crushed, smashed to smithereens. We may grow up in a ghetto during the Dust Bowl era, during wartime, or have parents who are unfit or only partially fit.

Our parents may wish us to be different than who we are, not attuned to us, their unfinished business and expectations spreading over us like an inky black cloud. We may be raised without nurturing, the feminine (not female) qualities of tenderness and comforting deficient. We may feel the pressure and limits of our time, gender, or culture.

We may be taught that god is a man in the sky or that there is no god. All the while, our little bodies and brains are developing, wiring, tuning. Regardless, we have a journey to travel, one that takes us from birth to death. A journey with the opportunity to discover who we are, to develop more of who we are. A journey through darkness to find the diamond of the self.

Crushed

As a child, I saw a kaleidoscope of life and death all around me. The green bud, the dead baby bird fallen from its nest. I experienced my parents' turmoil – their own guidance systems tangled with their histories. My father's explosive rage. Both my mother's desire to protect us and her meanness towards us. I experienced not only love but jealousy and, rage, pain, and confusion. In a sense, I lived suppressed by our family dynamics in a cloud of fear and uncertainty.

One day, my mother was angry. I am four years old. I do not remember why, or even if I knew why. We are upstairs in our first house in New Jersey. I have an articulating wood snake that was purchased at the World's Fair. I love this snake, how the joints move, its primitive look, its painted-on eyes. My mother grabs my snake and throws it out of the window. I am shocked, afraid, horrified.

As I think back, I realize there were deep stresses between my parents. My father sometimes went to bars and came back late. My mother had four children under the age of four. She had too much to hold, to manage. This stress was like an underground fissure, like lava or steam that needed to be released periodically. I felt this, was the recipient at times, but didn't understand it.

What is it like before we know who we are? What is it like being a child in an insensitive world? What is it like loving animals, pets, other people but not being able to intervene to make their lives better? What is it like to watch the suffering of those you love? I was crushed by this. Crushed because I yearned for peace and happiness. Because I felt what my animal friends felt. Just the other day, a friend who had recently been vaccinated stopped over. She was in a fog. I immediately felt a fog descend over me. What happens to those of us who can FEEL?

Malleable, I shifted and conformed to survive. I did not have my sister's strong fighting spirit, which I ceaselessly admire. I acquiesced, terrified and disturbed. I split the world into good and bad, victim and persecutor. I compensated by being overly kind, seeing the bully in my father but not the hurt child inside.

Later in life, I got caught in scenarios where I attempted to rescue people who were not my job to rescue, that I did not have the power to save. Caught in the need to help the perceived victim, I didn't know how to walk away. I was trying to soothe the part of them that was never soothed in me. It doesn't work that way. Those people had to decide they wanted to heal. Eventually, over time, I went back again and again and helped my traumatized inner child find her place. I soothed her and helped her feel held. I did for myself what hadn't been done for me when I was growing up.

Seed

Despite my confusion and my fear, my heart was strong, big. Still, I didn't know what my life wanted of me. I didn't know why I was here, what the purpose of my life would become. I didn't know who I was or that I was on the outer edge of sensitivity. Navigating through my feelings was difficult. They pushed and pulled me. They drove me in and out of the situations of my life. At the same time, a part of me was seeking. Those two drives, the velocity of my emotional needs and my search for meaning knotted together, leaving me unable to fully navigate. The chaos and uncertainty of my life scared me. I did not feel safe.

The pressures I grew up under, the version of myself I created to survive, were the beginning of the formation of the diamond I would become. Those pressures leave us with shame about who we are. As we learn to release those ways of survival, facets form and shift, allowing the beginnings of the formation of a strong being who can transmit light.

I did not know I was only a small plant, that I would become a large spreading tree. I did not know that I would mature and become capable. I did not know my potential. But I began to grow. And here I am.

✺

Choice

Two stories side by side.
One golden and bright
the other dim.

I step out
of the story of history
and into my future.

I step out
of crooked perception
the skewed world
created by struggle, trauma.

I step into
the prism of sight
the rainbow splashed
celebrating
like a field of flowers.

Seeing the Gift

"Why did you let that happen? Why didn't you stop him? You could have blocked your brother with your body and saved the chick." My mother's words were harsh, the situation harsher.

With tears streaming down my face, my sister, myself, and my two brothers stood around my mother. We watched the baby pheasant lying on her cupped palm, its little eyes closed, a loop of glistening intestines burst through its abdomen. We watched its tiny body rising and falling, watched its breathing, in and out, rapid, and then stilled.

I am maybe eight years old. A local farmer had been mowing a nearby field and ran over and killed a mother pheasant sitting on her eggs. How we found out, I have no idea, but we took the eggs and put them under one of our nesting chickens. Although the eggs hatched, this particular chicken was not a great mother. The baby pheasants began to disappear each night, one by one. We took the last one away from the chicken to raise ourselves. This happy ball of golden fuzz was a part of our family for a short while.

Tragedy

One day, I took the baby chick out of its box and was lying in the grass beside it, enjoying the sunshine. It was a sweet little bird with a dark stripe over its eye. It happily peeped as it pecked at the grass. My little brother, who was four years old or so, came running towards me. Frozen, I saw what was to happen in slow motion. I yelled. Stop, stop, stop. Stoooooopppp. He continued running and stepped directly on the baby bird. No no no no no no.

The shock vibrated through me. I don't remember what happened next. I only remember it lying on my mother's palm as we watched it die. And I remember the blame.

I questioned myself: *Why had I let this happen? Why hadn't I reacted faster?* I was a sensitive, imaginative, and intuitive child who loved animals. I could easily experience their pain, merge with them, and lose my separate self.

What is a shadow? The dark field cast by someone or something standing between an object and a source of light. A shadow is a metaphor. And it is real. Love is the light. Blame creates a shadow. Growing up, we do not see the shadows cast upon us by those around us. We do not see how we are being impacted. Until later. We just know when we hurt, when we feel loved, when we don't feel respected or understood, or when we do feel these things.

No Support

It was rural Pennsylvania in the 60's. Our family had not yet reached the apex of stress that hit when my siblings and I were in our teenage years. We didn't really fit into this community of farmers and hunters. My mother's friends were still in New Jersey. I think my father's focus on his art left her lonely.

My father knew he would be an artist as a small boy. He was driven, heading out to his studio in the morning, taking a break for lunch and dinner, and often returning to his studio at night. He did not have the support of his parents for his life's path and work.

While he was a very prolific and esteemed science fiction illustrator – illustrating the works of Robert A. Heinlein, Isaac Asimov, and many others, as well as magazines such as Analog, he ached for his fine art, his drawings, paintings, and sculptures to be seen and known, his true brilliance to be recognized. His imagination and creativity were vast, and I was filled with awe. This split between the work he did for money and the work he did for love eventually healed as he was able to acknowledge the value of his illustrations, but during my time growing up, it was a raw wound, a yearning, and the source of pain. It was one of the wounds that clouded his magnificent spirit.

My parents did not have support from their community, relatives, or even fully from each other. Nor did they know how to emotionally support their children. Each of us held our individual selves up as best as we were able. We were a family who saw ourselves through the lens of free will. Each expected to be independent and separate rather than interdependent. We were not a family that understood the concept of a higher will or had faith. We did not understand nurturing or emotional support or how necessary those qualities were for us to develop and function. This meant not only that I felt and was considered responsible for what happened but that I had to get through this trauma by myself. That I was traumatized was not even recognized.

My mother was an emotionally distant person. She undoubtedly had what used to be called Asperger's, now called Autism Spectrum Disorder. Growing up, there were no hugs, no "I'm so sorry, it wasn't your fault. I know you are sad." There was no reassurance, emotional nurturing, or help in understanding what had occurred.

My father, while at times fun and jovial, had dark moments and could move into rage and meanness. We were seen as children in that we had to obey, and adult in that we had to take care of ourselves emotionally with nobody to lean into but ourselves.

※

Held

Hold me
in your hand.

Cup me
in your palm.

Love me
through it all.

Free Fall

When we are held and comforted, the body relaxes and loosens, the mind stills. The breath softens. That is what I needed but did not get. Instead, I was thrown into an existential state where I was alone. Like a nuclear explosion, this accident ballooned and vibrated through my psyche with no exit. At eight or nine, I simply did not have the internal resources to grieve and let go. Who do you blame in a situation like this? A four-year-old? The farmer who killed the nesting pheasant with his plow? Us for saving the developing eggs? Me for not knowing to throw my body over the baby bird to protect it?

I couldn't deal with what happened by myself. I didn't have the capacity. Without support, I merged with the body shock and trauma this little bird experienced. I could not see beyond it. I free-fell into the dark pit of self-blame, my mind spinning. And I moved into even greater hypervigilance afterward.

The image of the little pheasant as it died on my mother's cupped palm has haunted me for more than fifty years. It has been one of the places inside where I have not trusted the universe, where I struggle to believe the world is good. It is where I was blamed, and I blamed myself. When the suffering is too intense, we often fall into blame. How do we untangle the trauma, the blame, and the guilt? How do we heal trauma? And yet, this darkness within which I grew, within which I was shrouded, this darkness of blame, held the capacity to heal, to make whole, to form a new being who could see the world differently, with new eyes.

A Happening

I've always struggled with "accidents." In my life, accidents have often been connected to trauma. And they have impacted my ability to trust that the universe is safe. What is the relationship between an accident and what is meant to be, or destiny? I've wondered about this for my entire life. Are there accidents? One theory I've read puts forth the idea that when your energy is out of balance, accidents can happen. Others indicate that there is no such thing as an accident.

I, of course, have feelings about this. On the one hand, I want to believe that everything is meaningful. The idea of an accident makes me feel unsafe. On the other hand, I struggle with so many horrific events in our world. If there are no accidents, then what is this place? How do we create meaning around what happens?

One way I have dealt with this is to believe in reincarnation. To believe that all is experience. That trauma can be healed. That we can heal. That we can learn and grow. That in the holographic field that is existence, we move in and out of different situations. In and out of other dimensions. In and out of different lives. Still, I have struggled with the idea of accident, with what seems like the unfairness of it.

In the dictionary, an accident is "an unfortunate incident that happens unexpectedly and unintentionally, typically resulting in damage or injury." It is "'a happening,' from the verb accidere, from ad- 'towards, to' + cadere 'to fall.'"

A falling towards a happening. I see it as indicating a fall from grace.

A fall into the deep underbelly of darkness, where light does not exist or cannot be found. Where we are alone and without connection to others or our own divinity. And yet, it is from contrast that we see both light and dark. From the struggle, we turn our heads towards what is light and begin to move towards it, building it into our being.

Spirit Medicine

Once, years ago, I tried 5-MeO-DMT (which is different from straight DMT. The effects are much more powerful. Both 5-MeO-DMT and DMT are found in ayahuasca, which also has other compounds and alkalines) with my shaman friend, Otto. Ayahuasca is a plant-based psychoactive decoction. One of its uses is as a ceremonial, spiritual medicine among indigenous peoples from the Amazon basin.

I went straight to hell, to a place with no light, no love, no god. A place with skeletal beings and demons. The forty-five minutes of this experience seemed to last for days. I clutched Otto's arm in desperate terror. When I finally emerged, I was so grateful to be back in ordinary reality, to be with my friend and his cats. An appreciation I did not fully see before this descent.

It took years for me to integrate this experience. Eventually, as I looked back, I saw how my fear of death had evaporated. In my DMT experience, I had already been somewhere worse than death. I had been to the underworld in its darkest form. I also saw how much fear I had, how it was an underlayer of my consciousness. That layer of fear has been released, transmuted. Instead, I am more informed by trust.

Underbelly

In Greek mythology, the underworld was usually not returned from. But some did manage to descend to that realm and return to the living world. The journey to the underworld undoubtedly gave the traveller a gift - whether it was a loved one, a powerful object, an extraordinary skill, or knowledge. The ability to enter this realm while living and return spoke of a certain kind of mastery.

This ability is one of the talents of a witch, shaman, or sorcerer. Again, the pejorative enters here with the idea of conjuring evil spirits instead of having the talent to descend and return with new gifts, gifts of healing that only those who have survived the dark can have.

I've experienced descent into the underworld in a variety of ways. From the traumatic incident of the pheasant chick to the immersion in the DMT trip, to years spent in a relationship with a person addicted to drugs, me addicted to that person, to years struggling with the hopelessness of a debilitating illness, these underworld experiences are linked.

With the DMT trip, I went down and came back up. The gold to be gained from that experience, while still years away, was percolating deep in my psyche.

Debilitating illness often precipitates a sense of both false hope and hopelessness. There is a descent before one surfaces with more understanding and perspective. A few years after I became very ill, and even more years before I was diagnosed with Lyme disease,

I was still caught in the belief that this illness was temporary, that I would regain the physical self I had before I got sick. I hadn't yet realized, much less accepted, that this disease was a journey. I hadn't yet realized that this journey would teach me and that my illness was a natural consequence of who I was when I got sick. I still, at times, buck against this knowing. But before I emerged into this knowing, I plummeted into the murky world of despair. With this disease, problematic relationships, and other difficult chapters of my life, I had entered a nightmare.

To emerge into a brighter world, I had to change. I had to become different - engage with myself and reality in new ways. These dark "chapters" of suffering are somewhat different than an event that erupts into our lives in the form of trauma. An eruption shakes us apart in a moment. A dark chapter occurs over a long period and slowly dismantles who we are. But there are also similarities.

Relating to Reality

When we have an untenable experience, whether an accident or not, whether brief and acute or chronic and over a long period, we need to find ways to hold ourselves together. In a sense, the experience becomes frozen in our nervous system. There is work to be done to release ourselves from this prison. To make use of these experiences, we need to seek meaning and find a more enlightened way of engaging with life.

When I was much younger and in a relationship with a man with a severe addiction, I learned that I was "co-dependent" with him in a way that caused me harm.

Al-Anon not only helped me build the backbone I did not have but introduced me to the idea that I was not in control, that there were forces more significant than me. With these new learnings, I began to develop and practice new ways of relating to reality.

As I look at the seemingly unfortunate and accidental events of my life, some of them clearly occurred because I needed to change course. These "accidents" are easier to accept because I can see their purpose. It is those that seemingly have no purpose that I find more challenging. We live in a world of free will where our choices may cause another harm, sometimes in the form of an accident, and a world that is at times dangerous, although in the larger field of reality and in the context of reincarnation, it is all part of experience. It is all part of finding our strength, our light. Accident or not.

Transmuting Trauma

In 2019, I spent some time doing EMDR [Eye Movement Desensitization and Reprocessing] with a therapist. I went because I felt I needed to heal past experiences that affected my sense of safety at a bedrock level and thereby impacted my sleep. Dr. Arielle Schwartz states, "EMDR Therapy changes maladaptive neural networks by connecting the traumatic memory with new information. The distressing thoughts and emotions are blended with new positive thoughts and emotions; embodied awareness allows frozen sensations in the body to resolve through healing movements."

I found the process of EMDR awkward and uncomfortable but valuable.

I entered Steven's office and sat down across from him. He had initially spent an entire session getting an idea of the events I felt were traumatic and assessing my ability to self-support, to return to an integrated and functional state after our work together and before I left his office. He made sure I had an internal safe place and the ability to leave the traumatic state behind when I needed to return to my "regular" life. The point is to be able to alter the trauma so it no longer envelopes the person, so it fades to the background and transforms into an experience that no longer takes over.

And then we began. We would pick an event, and as Steven moved a ball back and forth and my eyes followed, I would think of that event. Steven would ask me what was happening, what I was experiencing. Over and over. The event morphed until it became something different. Until, instead of feeling like a victim of my father's rage or my mother's control, I found a new vision, an image of my empowerment. Instead of cowering, I confronted. My emotional responses changed, and new internal experiences emerged.

Throughout ten or so sessions, we moved through many "bad" memories – memories that had stayed with me for decades and caused me a sense of pain and a perception of feeling powerless and unsafe. Traumatic memories and traumatic states of being are not empowered places. I don't know what shifted internally, but at some point, I realized I had more ground under my feet. There was a bottom supporting me. An intangible fear I had carried for years had diminished. There was more space in my psyche now for empowerment and light.

I had forgotten the story of the baby peasant when I was working with Steven. It wasn't one of the situations we entered and transformed. Yet now, I am finding a new place to stand in relation to this event. I am healing from that trauma, and those messages of blame and disempowerment connected to that event. I am finding a new vista that is more light-filled. The nightmare fades and becomes an event I stand further from, with a different perspective. It no longer destroys me as it did.

✶

Blooms

The Tulip
fringe-lipped or modest and plain
emerges in spring.

Somehow it knows
what time it is
and shares its simple beauty.

✶

Magic Blooms

I live in a world where the universe evolves with beauty, and magic blooms at the edges of my vision. Where I know I create my life, and I stand in that power. I live in a world where I know I have a purpose and a mission.

Which world do I wish to live in? Knowing the answer is easy. Turning my naturally obsessive gaze from the problem to the solution is much more difficult. Daily, we are confronted with the choice of how we direct our energy and what we are creating or honoring. As someone I know once said to me, "Take the needle out of your arm." She was referring to my obsession with trying to solve problems at the problem level instead of taking care of myself. Instead of setting an intention, doing the work required, and then allowing the universe to do its job.

I can turn from my obsession with trying to control outcomes as an attempt to feel safe and find other ways of relating to the universe. I tell myself that I am developing as a human. That I am gifted by the many beautiful beings around me. That I can find faith and love. That I can make my path more joyful and live in balance. That I can practice these ways.

I trust that my vision will come to pass if it is in alignment with the universe's will and that this journey has changed me for the better. This journey is more expansive than my will. My engagement with this journey is where my power lies. My task is to live with joy even as I am confronted with obstacles, accidents, challenges. My task is also to heal from trauma. To do so, I require support, both internal and external.

Extreme Kindness

A new knowing has emerged, a new vision; my world contains extreme kindness. My siblings, mother, and I gathered to witness with love as the chick's inhales and exhales ceased. We buried him or her. We cried. Although we were not then aware, in this circle of love, there was a gift to all of us. That gift stood side by side with the shock, pain, grief, and blame. It is as if there were two different realities. The golden moment of sharing and honoring stood side by side with blame and trauma – like the contrast between the good witch and the bad witch in The Wizard of Oz. We had fallen into the clutches of the bad witch; we did not realize the perspective of the good witch. We were looking through the wrong eyes. The door to seeing that circle of love was not open to me until recently.

Now, I have the opportunity to unhook these two things, to unhook the blame and shock from the grief and love. I have the chance to release the blame, the guilt, the pain, and maybe even heal the trauma. Now, I can see love, too, in that tragedy.

How often do we get caught in trauma and tragedy instead of in beauty? How do we accept adversity and choose to see what is beautiful? Every day, heinous acts take place. Every day, miracles occur. The universe is alive. Right now. Choose to draw to yourself the support you need, the support that is available to you. Get on the path to healing trauma. Walk through your fears and find whatever calls you. There are so many ways: meditation, therapy, workshops, books, journaling, writing groups.

Circle of Love

That little bird died surrounded by love. He passed quickly. I chose to release the trauma, allow the grief, and find the beauty. His short life impacted all of us. We wanted him to live, to enjoy, to have a full, happy pheasant life. We cherished and enjoyed his little downy body, his little happy peeps as we watched him peck grass. In the accident, our circle of love was lost. That, too, was tragic. But in the healing, that circle reformed.

Healing

Do you see how the darkness you have lived through has allowed you to move into the light? To move from aloneness to interconnection? How I grew and healed is how you can also grow and heal.

Our lives circle back again and again. Like the movement of the seasons. There is an opportunity to gain clarity with each revolution. To find more of ourselves and connect with love to those around us. To be inhabited by more light. To begin to know who we are and what we are capable of. We learn to stand in a place of vision and healing. We find our inner knowing and our power.

✺

3
Descent

Where you stumble and fall, there you will find gold.
~ Joseph Campbell

Relinquish

I went out into the world broken. And because I was not fully formed, because I formed in a crooked way, I could not navigate. I had not developed the ability to self-navigate. I did not have the ability to say no, to choose myself first in certain areas. Career, yes. Relationships, no. My father was the one with charisma, with power in our family. My mother more subservient to his needs. And because of this, because of what I saw in our family, I was attached more to what was masculine rather than the feminine. I saw the power of the masculine, and so my own feminine side was present but unrecognized, unacknowledged, and unaffirmed by me. I had no real access to my deep feminine self.

And I felt more than my own suffering. I could feel your suffering more strongly than my own.

I was willing to sacrifice myself so others would be soothed. I was willing to take less so you could have more.

While this can be noble in a strong and grounded person, for me, I could not take enough to nourish myself.

I also had an addiction. The addiction to the feeling of love. To the men who could give me that feeling. My unfed inner child craved adoration, but she could not captain our ship in the waters of love. Blind, she drove me straight into the rocks.

Pulled Under

My second boyfriend, whom I live with, has just broken up with me. I am at the restaurant where I work as a waitress. I am sobbing. We have had some struggles. An artist, he is obsessed with photographing beautiful, sexy women. I am attractive. I do not consider myself beautiful. Nor does he, for he does not photograph me. I must ask him, request that he also do a photo shoot of me. I have begun to get upset with him for this behavior. I feel unloved, not valued. I had started to question him, put pressure on him around what I see as an obsession that robs our relationship. A co-worker who is my friend is with me. She is trying to soothe me, calm me down, help me know I will be okay, that I will survive this. I feel I will not. Pain pulsates through me. I can barely breathe. I do not understand what has happened, why he has pushed me away. I cannot see past the pain I am in. I do not see my value, only his rejection of my need and desire for a more fully functioning relationship.

When light shines through a crystal or prism, the breadth of the rainbow is affected by the density of the material. Similarly, whatever powers, talents, or abilities a person has, they cannot operate gracefully through the density of that structure. Their luminosity cannot fully shine through and is caught in a bend, refracted, instead of standing straight. Because of this, because this was me, life grabbed me and pulled me under. Underwater into the deep grays, murky browns, and muted greens of desperate and festering feelings.

Under to where I could not see clearly, where I did not have power, where I could not find my fire.

To rebuild myself, I would have to dive down into my subconscious to relinquish my attachment to what I saw as more valuable and powerful. I would have to descend through mishaps and suffering until I recognized the power of the feminine and claimed it as my own. I would have to claim my body as beautiful, not shameful. Claim my anger as useful, not dangerous, use my compassion without it bringing me down, and understand the inner journey as more valuable than the outer, even as they danced together. It was as if the imprint of my mother, the caretaker who self-sacrificed for her family, and my father, the authoritarian who held the power, had seeped into me like a stain I could not erase. These imprints were part of my very structure, part of the density of my being.

Murky Waters

The descent into the underworld of weaknesses and bad decisions can be a prelude to a fractured life. Or it can be a wake-up call, the beginning of what will lead to becoming conscious. This time spent in the murky waters of spiritual crisis is sometimes referred to as the dark night of the soul. We are pulled down into darkness until, gasping for air, we decide to accept the challenge, restructure the self, and, in some cases, open our psychic eyes.

My descent included experiences I was ashamed of. Experiences that many people would have judged, had they known; getting pregnant, loving a man who could not be there for me, my difficulty holding boundaries, my inability to truly take care of myself.

These experiences compiled, piled up like wave after wave crashing onto the rocks. I saw myself then. Saw my small, damaged body wrecked on the shore. Saw that only I could save myself. I reached out. Grabbed onto whatever I could. This would not be my final fate. This would not be the story of my life.

But first, I had to say to myself, "I am broken. There is something wrong with me." Then I could begin to rebuild, to bring myself back.

✵

Fire

We are young.
Our elderly neighbors have raked
the dry fall leaves into big piles.
My siblings and I jump in them, laughing.
Then, they are burned.

We watch transfixed
as the orange fire jumps upward.
The fire goblins race about.
Fire leaping, licking the sky.
Smoke swirling upward.
The magic of fire, of transformation,
the leaves blackening, crumpling
as the fire dances.
Release from form.
What was is no longer.

Blood

My life had reached a really bad point. It was spring 1990. I had been with this man for less than a year. I came home after a twelve-hour day of work. My boyfriend was smoking crack in my apartment. He knew better. He knew to not bring it into the apartment.

"Don't bring it into my home. I do not want to see it."
He was sitting on the bed with his pipe. I grabbed at his hand.
"Give it to me."
"No, leave me alone. You'll get hurt."
I wouldn't stop. All the time, I had coached him on stopping. Wasted. We wrestled for the pipe.
"Give it to me. You know I hate this," I screamed.

We struggled. Snap. It broke. Sliced through my hand. I stopped and stared at my hand, at the cut that had sliced my palm open, at red blood oozing out.

He walked into the bathroom to finish smoking, left me bleeding. How had my life come to this?

Burnt

When I tried to wrestle the crack pipe from my boyfriend's hand, I was wrestling with his destiny, not mine. My will would not make his struggle go away. My will was not aligned with what he needed to confront in himself, the choice he needed to make. He needed to decide that life was worth living, that the feelings he had, lurking, crying under the surface, were worth digging up and healing.

He had to decide that he wanted more than a life of addiction, that he was worth more.

When I tried to wrestle the crack pipe from him because I wanted him, his love, the attention of his soft brown eyes, I was too close to his fire. I tried to stop something that I had no business with. I got burnt by his flame.

I also had to look at my addiction to love. What was I trying to hold onto, to pull into myself? How could I find self-love instead of grasping at love from someone who could not put me first, whose first love was his relationship with being high? Who was this hungry, desperate girl? How would I feed her, nurture her, help her grow up, strengthen, and find her power? How would she learn to stand on her own two feet and claim the abilities that were hers?

✵

My Camera

Months later, I opened a cabinet in my apartment. My camera was gone.

I was never much good at speaking. Just didn't know how to say clean and clear how I felt. I'd always just stand there, mouth locked shut. And I'd end up bawling with everyone thinking I was dumb. But at least I had my camera tucked away in the closet and knew it was there. I loved it. It was mine.

How could you? Mine, mine, mine. It was given to me, a gift. The second favorite thing I ever had. Specks, my horse, was my first, and I loved him the best, but he was already gone. But my camera. Don't you know that I'm nothing without my camera? Don't you know that? And you sold it, blew it up your nose, smoked it in a pipe. Burned my camera away. My camera. The part of me that spoke for me, that said all that could not be put into words, that made the world beautiful, neat. And I could say something with it.

My camera, black with buttons and knobs. I could make beauty out of a pile of dead leaves lying abandoned on a sidewalk at night. And the hole in my heart just got bigger, and I don't know where to go, how to stop this life out of control.

My camera. I was special with it. Now I am a woman stolen from again, with a chasm so big I don't know where to put it. My camera made me more than two long skinny legs and arms and large clumsy head.

My camera. And then it was gone. I opened the cupboard. Gone.

I knew. You had taken it. You, who I love. You did it. My scream is deep in my throat.

Too deep to ever come out. It is locked away. You who I love, the brown curl of your lashes, the tightness of your hug, the need of your voice.

You, you stole it.

My camera.

The Key

It was the morning two days after we fought over the pipe, and I knew what I would do. As we left the apartment together, I turned towards him and said, "Give me the key." Ice cold.

He did not argue. I took it. Cold metal. Hard. I shut the door, turned the key, listened to the lock click into place.

He stood in the hallway staring at me with his large, beautiful brown eyes.

"Good luck," I said as I walked away. I was ready to let him die. I doubted I would ever see him again.

The boundary falls into place when it is time, when it is ready. The million bad things that had happened in the year I spent with this man; I had not kicked him out alone. By now, I had been in Al-Anon for six months. I didn't make this decision.

This decision made itself, and I was there to witness and enact it. It made itself because I had taken the steps needed, built the internal structure required so that a part of me could stand strong, find my voice, take another step toward health.

An Ocean Away

He was in rehab. He found a friend to help him get admitted a day after I kicked him out. He asked me to attend family week. Addicts and their families gathered. I sat there, a roomful of strangers away, separated by all the broken promises and hurt feelings between us.

We were told to ask for forgiveness from each other for all the wrongs we had done to each other. For the hurtful acts, for being mean, lying, accusing, yelling, screaming, controlling. I had done my share of that while he was not fully alive, while he was living only on the compulsion to use. I had done that because I hadn't recognized that he could not help himself, that he wasn't intentionally hurting me. That the lying and stealing were about the state of his addiction, not about me.

I sat there and looked across at him. I spoke, "You feel an ocean away from me now. I feel safe this far away, miles and miles of cool, calm ocean between us. I don't feel you. I don't need you. I am afraid to come closer and be trapped again. I don't want to come across this ocean between us. I am happier over here, away from you."

He sat looking at me, and I could see an emptiness inside him. Then he spoke, "Please don't leave me now. I need you. I think of you, and knowing you are there helps me keep going."

A heaviness descended on me. I knew what he said was true and that I could not go yet. He still needed me, and because of this, I could not leave him.

I had more inner work to do, more 12-step meetings, more journaling, more learning. It would be another three and a half years before I would be strong enough to leave for good.

Eyes Open

It was he who showed me the impact of my past. He who forced my eyes open to see something was terribly wrong with me. It was because of my struggle with him that I had to look at myself and see what had been and why I had been left so crippled, and what I had to do to both survive my past and overcome it. It was he who made me ask myself, "What is wrong with me?" This relationship initiated the beginning of my self-directed path of awakening. I was twenty-nine years old.

※

Follow Bliss

Today. Outside. Swirling colors.
Bush and branch. Bird and trunk. Sky and cloud.

Seasons change.
Warm, Cold. White, Gold, Green.
Daily, I pick up my colors, my thoughts, my palette.
My life is my art.
I follow love.
I feel joy.

I release what I cannot do, cannot control.
My mind focuses on what is.
I create a heaven.
I know my mission.
Why I am here.

�֎

New World

It is 2008, and I am in a session with Ellen, the Soul Memory Discovery master teacher and practitioner. She is very stern. She says, "STOP. Stop what you are doing. Stop." She tells me she never gets directives like this from the guides. This never happens. I do not yet know why my guides are saying this, what she means. I do not yet understand. I do not yet see what I am doing to myself. I do not yet see the intensity of my fear, how I am hurting myself. I have not yet fallen this time.

2009, I find myself feeling overwhelmed. I am in the middle of juggling big challenges in my life. I have lost my perspective. I am sick. I am moving. I am remodeling my house to get it ready to rent. I am figuring out how to change my psychotherapy practice so I can continue to see clients, even as I move two hours away. I try to push through these changes, this chapter of my life, so I can move on to what is next, which, in my imagination, can only be better. My pushing comes out of fear, of not trusting. Instead of recognizing and being in what it is, I am trying to make my life something it isn't. I realize that I have little control over the events occurring around me; I know I am stuck. Although I am aware of feeling triggered and how my anxiety and control relate to my past – the legacy of fear and caution I inherited, I am unable to find another way to see things and move into a more empowered position on my own. I cannot be kind to myself because I am steeped in fear and not trusting that I will get through the current challenges.

I take the issue to my therapist. She gives me a different way of looking at what is occurring and helps me see what I am trying to learn, what my life is trying to teach me.

She helps me see the need to be kinder to myself, to guide myself out of self-kindness instead of fear. Because of this, I am able to make different choices in how I perceive what is happening and in how I relate to the events in my life. I see how I need to let go of the external as a way of evaluating myself and focus on my internal worth. I start to let go of the struggle that I am in. I begin to say to myself:

Although I do not feel safe and am uncomfortable, I am safe.

I am trying to control the uncontrollable.

I refuse to do that and ruin my day.

How I use my energy in this moment is more important than where I think I am headed.

I will not misuse my energy (get tense, hopeless, etc.) because it will only perpetuate my chaos.

I choose joy, grace, and dignity because I can.

I will not allow external circumstances to dictate my mood, how I use my energy, who I am.

Tuning In

Working with the pendulum means allowing it to swing, giving me yesses and nos according to the direction it moves. For me, a yes answer occurs when the pendulum moves counterclockwise. When it swings toward and away from me, the answer is a no. As it moves, I also often hear words, sentences. As I work with the pendulum and tune in, I am reminded by my guides to notice my energy in each moment. What am I doing with it? What are my thoughts? What do I tell myself?

I am shifting. Plenty of things are not going the way I want them to, but I no longer allow this to derail me. Instead, I am feeling better, more empowered, more accepting of the imperfections of life.

As I engage in this process of transforming myself, I begin to ask, "What about me?" "What is life whispering in my ear?" "What is my life trying to teach me?" I begin to see how important it is for me to trust the happenings of my life.

Aligning

I get to choose the lens I look through. What if I decided that my life is my friend? What if I choose to see that absolutely everything in my life is purposeful and designed to help me evolve? I know that the only way I can become who I most want to be - joyous, grateful, trusting - is by deciding that absolutely everything that is happening to me, everything in my life, is in support of my growth.

Because I want to trust my life, I choose to. Not once but over and over, as challenges arise and throw me into doubt for a moment, an hour, or a day, I tell myself, *"I trust my life. My life is my friend. The events in my life assist me in my growth and evolution."* I seek ways to see what my life is trying to tell me so that I can cooperate with it rather than fight against it.

The Opening Door

I can now generate positivity rather than staying mired in negativity. Slowly, as I focus on my energy, on reforming myself, as I correct deficits in myself, my structure changes. I become not the footprint to my father's foot, the imprint to another's form, but a being who has weight and takes space.

This process, this inner exploration, and honoring the full self, not just what society deems important, will reveal more internal obstacles to be moved through and open the door to self-love and self-empowerment. There is velocity in this process. The road smoother and smoother. A path moving into ease and grace, the result of grappling fully with my descent. A path that allowed me to find more of myself, my knowing, my I AM witch self.

✷

4
Bringing Myself Back

We all begin as a bundle of bones lost somewhere in a desert, a dismantled skeleton that lies under the sand. It is our work to recover the parts. It is a painstaking process best done when the shadows are just right, for it takes much looking.
~ Clarissa Pinkola Estés, Ph.D.

※

Broken Girl

I am a broken girl, and I know it. It is 1990, and I stare at the wall in my apartment, sobbing. I am distraught, and everything in my life feels wrong. Piled up like dark shadows are the many events that have felt harmful. My entanglement with Eric, a man I love who is out of control, the distress of an unwanted pregnancy and abortion, the anxiety I am wrapped in. I must find a way to bring myself back. Out of this despair. Out of the shadow world of addiction and co-dependence, back into a world where I can function in relationships, where I can say no. Where my legs and arms work. Where the choices I make enlarge rather than compress my life.

I have not only to function but find the magic of myself and my life. I have to find my power.

I seek help for my brokenness. My soul, my presence, my inner self no longer want to be trapped in a person who cannot navigate through my emotional world.

A drive emerges. I will fix myself. This drive moves me through self-work, 12-step work, years of therapy, and, later in life, therapeutic training. I am hungry to be whole. I am hungry to be a full person.

I find myself in a therapy group for co-dependents – briefly, maybe three sessions. This was as I began my 12-step work. We sat together, four other women, me, and a therapist. I could hear how stuck they were, we were. The therapist talked of the addict as evil, saying we deserved someone better. I knew he was wrong. I knew Eric was not evil, though he lied to me, hurt me, and was very sick. And I knew I did not deserve better. I knew I had to be in that relationship until I was capable of being somewhere else. I knew that looking at Eric as the enemy would stop me. I knew the enemy was deep inside me. I knew it was my past.

Bringing Myself Back

I did not know I was a witch when I was younger. I only knew I was excruciatingly sensitive – seemingly to my detriment. It was only when life forced me to deal with my brokenness that I started on the journey to healing myself and began to be able to manifest my potential. We don't always take this journey. Sometimes, we get caught in the mirage that only the external is real and is exclusively where our focus needs to be.

We may lose sight of the value of inner exploration and so settle for a much smaller world and more limited possibilities for ourselves.

Bringing myself back was a very early stage of healing, for healing occurs on a continuum.

To heal is to make whole. For me, it was to take my fragmented self, my self that was weak and caught, and become someone who stood in her own power, who was able to stand independently and not sacrifice herself to the hungry ghost of another person's addiction.

✺

Bones

I did not know
how the universe would hold me.

That it is peopled, populated, pulsing.

I did not know what to reach for,
what to hold.

I did not know I needed bones,
or how to grow them.

I did not know
my nourishment
would come from other worlds
and from myself.

My bones have become strong
as I have become bigger.

My bones gleam
in the night.

My bones hold.

Bones That Hold

After I crashed and burned, I began to grab at the threads that would save me. The idea that it wasn't all up to me. The calling in of other perspectives. The beginning of untangling myself from ways of being that harmed me. The learning to calm down anxiety and fear. The trusting that I did not have to rescue every hurt being I loved, for I felt compelled to take care of those I saw suffering. I began to realize that some of them had their own work to do. That my obsession with them kept both of us stuck. It kept them from grappling with and taking responsibility for who they were and deciding who they wanted to become.

I began to repair my brokenness. I began to do the therapeutic work that would allow me to grow into a functioning human. I began to unwind my anxiety so I could hear my intuition, which had been lost in the swirling fears. I began to develop better boundaries and learn to differentiate between my feelings and yours. I began to have the space to make better choices. Synchronicities put specific learning paths and books in front of me. I was guided through my healing in this way. I began to be able to say no. It took a long time to get my feet fully under me.

Later, I became facile in the healing process. Later, I could move back and forth from a functional and regular reality to the non-ordinary reality of inner psychodramas, stories, and myths to meet traumas, fractured parts of myself, disembodies aspects, and distortions. Eventually, my life smoothed out, and I began to feel integrated and solid instead of being caught in struggle. But for now, I would have to focus on growing new bones, strong bones, bones that gleamed and could hold flesh. Bones that held my body and did not collapse under the weight of being human.

Without Blinders

After we choose to bring ourselves back. After we look at ourselves without blinders and say, "*No, this will not be my life. I will find a way to grow beyond this life I have created.*" After we look at ourselves and say, "*No, this is not why I am here. This is not enough for me.*" After that, there is a long road.

Healing was vital to my having a fulfilling life. When we avoid healing, not only do we live in a discordant self – for our state of being is the home of our experience – but sooner or later, we will be confronted with what we pushed away... whether in a different chapter of life or a different life or reality.

The Gate Opens

This decision to bring myself back was an initiation of sorts. An opening of the gates to higher consciousness. Imagine a gate in your mind opening. As it opens, the light brightens. You feel a shift in your body. You feel lighter, more aware. Your world has changed.

The term initiation is mysterious. It indicates opening to or gaining instruction in the mysteries of sacred knowledge. We may think of the rites of passage of some tribal cultures where a young man goes through a difficult challenge requiring both courage and the ability to tolerate pain so that he may move from boyhood to manhood. We may think of the rites of a fraternity or sorority that change us from non-member to member. Or a ritual or ceremony that is part of becoming a practicing witch who is then in community with other witches.

Essentially, initiation refers to movement from one state of consciousness to another, usually through a challenge, trial, or struggle. Often led by a member of the group who has already passed through the gates of initiation. Sometimes initiation involves pain, physical and emotional. Sometimes it is violent. The ache of heartbreak. The scream of a body hurt. Other times, it occurs through the doorway of repairing trauma. Whether ecstatic, violent, or simply through challenge, these experiences open us, move us to another state of being, or expanded consciousness.

The Voice of Purpose

These transitions change us, change our consciousness. I remember a therapy session I did with a couple. They were struggling. But they also clearly shared a deep love. As they sat with me and talked, I clearly saw one partner's challenge. This man backed away from his relationship when it became difficult because his partner needed more. His insecurities entered and took over, telling him he wasn't enough, that things were wrong. I saw his purpose standing there next to him.

His purpose said, *"You are enough. You are bigger than your fears and insecurities. You are meant to step through them and be there for this person, help her heal from her trauma. Make that shift. Grab onto that understanding, and your relationship will get the nourishment it needs. You will find your strength, and she, her healing."*

I shared this with him. I saw him brighten; a gate cracked open as I spoke.

His relationship was an initiation that, should he choose to accept the challenge, would enable him to walk through an opening and become more conscious and empowered.

He would be able to provide much-needed support and feel his power and value in doing so.

A Living Initiation

My initiations came organically through what life handed me. Difficult situations that I had to overcome demanded I change. But to do so, I had to become a different and better version of myself. My initiatory experiences are very connected to my path of healing.

For me, initiation is not a formal ritual. It isn't joining a group and agreeing to their traditions. My commitment is to my inner self and to the divinity of the universe as I understand it. I don't concern myself with the steps of initiation or identifying where I might be. I am simply concerned with emotional, spiritual, and heart-centered self-mastery.

I've had to re-experience feelings and memories I would rather have avoided. But to reclaim these split-off parts, we may have to voyage into different ways of understanding ourselves. In a sense, we must travel to the underworld of ourselves. We journey to our wounded parts, parts that are terrified, splintered, or misshapen. Until we consciously do so, these parts may rise up, unbidden, and grab us. They are not part of our regular awareness, so we do not have control over them. Instead, unseen, they influence us, pull on us, cause us to act out, or cause us to become trapped in ways of being that do not serve us.

Shadow Work

We are often afraid of our underworld because we do not understand it. We are under the illusion that we can bypass what we do not want. That we choose can day and avoid night. That we can have life and push away death. That our lives should be about joy without the depth of struggle. We attempt to hold onto the light and do not see the value of darkness. Our lives flatten because we do not have dimension, and we fall victim to that which we do not claim. Working through our trauma, stepping out of the shadow is an essential process if we are to fully inhabit our light.

This work in the underworld is often called shadow work because we work with non-ordinary states of reality. We may be experiencing past life regression or working with inner images, releasing and transforming energies. Those of us who journey into the underworld to repair ourselves develop capacities that many people do not develop. I was called to go into the underworld and heal my trauma. I became a healing witch who could work in non-ordinary states of being, including the secret world of inner voices and split-off parts, of pushed away feelings and traumas, of Jungian archetypes and images.

The Fracture Repairs

Some modern-day witches and shamans can guide us to these places and help make us whole. They can help us understand and accept these wounded aspects, develop compassion for them, and ultimately integrate them into our psyche. They may be able to travel into interior worlds and make adjustments to themselves or others so that the fractures repair.

They may know how to work with inner voices and the imagination. They may know how to enter the cells of the body and alter what is there. They may breathe light into what is fragmented.

In 1993, I had a dream. I was riding my horse, Specks, who I had as a teenager, bareback across a raging river. It was deep, dark brown, and rough – the cold water wet on my legs, thighs, up to my lower hips. Specks was doing his best to swim. As he tried to swim across the wild creek, he could not keep his head above water, his head raising and falling back into the water. He was struggling to breathe; he was drowning.

I woke, sat up straight from that dream in a panic, crying. I knew Specks had just died in real life. I was haunted by the struggle as Specks drowned in the dream. I didn't know what happened in his real life, how he had died, if it had been a good death of old age or something else. I hadn't been able to protect him and make sure he was safe for the rest of his life. This hurt me the most.

Years after that dream, I attended a dream workshop that my then-therapist, Kelly, ran at her house. I remembered that dream and volunteered to work with it in front of the group. Kelly guided me as I entered the nightmare. I found myself with Specks as he was struggling. I was able to get him out of the river and to our barn. In my mind's eye, I left him warm, dry, and safe.

This did not change the fact that he had died. Instead, it created an energetic inner sanctum where he was cared for and felt cared for. I changed that inner image, the inner reality, from trauma to a peaceful transition.

The energy of his fear-filled death was healed. This enabled me to release the haunting this dream had left with me. I was able to relax and feel as if he was okay. I was able to trust that his transition was as it needed to be.

Opening the Gates

As witches, we may develop an alternate world in which we are also at home. When I get to know people now, I can often see their inner workings. I can see spiritual-psychological structure. I think of a woman whose primary self submerges and disappears when a trauma self emerges, a trauma self who wants to kill another or herself to stop the emotional pain she is in. A trauma self that is not part of her regular functioning self. Shadow work and healing trauma become second nature for us. Like the Moon and Death cards in the Tarot, or Pluto in astrology, or Hades and Hecate in mythology, these witches reside not just in regular reality but also in the underworld.

Initiation lets us know there are gates and thresholds in our development and self-mastery. That the gate must open to move through the threshold. That we have the power to open those gates. And in doing so, we become a fuller and more complete being.

Putting the Pieces Together

I remember when Eric, the boyfriend whose addiction and behavior caused me to attend Al-Anon, sat in his first and last couples therapy session with me. He was at that time "clean," but we were struggling in our relationship. Afterward, Eric said he would not continue. That night he wanted me to go to a concert with him. I refused. I knew we were close to finished.

I knew if he could not do the work of growing, of looking at what was going on between us and within himself, I would not continue to acquiesce, to take care of him. I remember his disappointment and shock that I said no.

Now, later in life, I have a strong sense of myself. I know what my talents and abilities are. I know what my mission is and why I am on the planet. I am assisted in fulfilling my mission in many ways. There are no big blocks or obstacles. Even though I still have health issues and sometimes need to work when I would much rather be in bed, I am able to focus past my discomfort and be happy about the work I am doing.

I sit at my computer, tired and feeling sick. But as I focus and the words come through and out my fingers onto the page, I eventually forget how I am feeling. I am able to enjoy the flow I find myself in. Enjoy knowing that I have the privilege of choosing my work, my words, my thoughts, my projects.

And so, I have descended into myself. I am here. I am doing what I was born to do. It will be.

✹

Spirit

Butterfly, colored powder-covered wings.
Flower to flower. Flutter, breathing.
Tongue sips. Here. There. Messenger from where?

Inspire - in breath.
The spirit enlivens, animates. Life-force radiating.
Life, Breath, Spirit.

The spirit disperses.
The body folds in on itself
and begins its disintegration.
Release. Death. Transformation.

Before the butterfly,
the caterpillar cocoon digests its old self.
Sleeping cells awaken.
The destruction of what is.

New cells multiply, new form, new structure,
a new being.
Now, it lives on nectar, not leaves.

Now it soars.

Building Ground

It is 1990. Somehow, I drag myself out of my life and into an Al-Anon meeting. I take the subway to the Upper West Side and sit in a room with a circle of metal chairs, holding mostly older women wearing large diamond rings. They talk about their children. Their children who were raised with so much privilege but somehow had failed at launching. These people are kind. But they are living a different life than me. They are older and wealthy. I am young, poor. I don't have a child with addiction issues. I have a boyfriend I can't release.

A boyfriend who got me pregnant. A boyfriend who gave me STDs. A boyfriend who stole from me. A boyfriend who cheated. A boyfriend who went out late in the night to buy crack. A boyfriend whose jaw crunched under a metal pipe wielded in the dark of Bedford–Stuyvesant late in the night. Me sitting in the emergency room with him, surrounded by blood, accident, and tragedy. Waiting as the gunshot victims and more serious injuries were attended to first. Surrounded by being in the wrong place at the wrong time. Surrounded by those trapped in the dark.

I was in love with him. My actions initiated a descent that would open me up to a new life. I tried to save this man caught in addiction who got me into the 12-step rooms, where I would later admit to myself that I was broken, that I needed to fix myself, that there was no other way for me to move forward. I would go to 12-step meetings, Al-Anon, Co-Anon, Nar-Anon, Adult Children of Alcoholics, Co-Dependence Anonymous, three times a week for three years and then less frequently for a number of years afterward.

I sit in these meetings. I listen, absorb. "Let Go and Let God." "First Things First." "One Day at a Time." I take in these thoughts. They still the anxiety threaded through me, the strands that tie me up, pull at me, twist me, contort. Nights I lay awake worrying. My mind spinning circles with no outlet. Where is he? Why hasn't he called me back? Is he safe? Crack dens, dim with stained mattresses, semi-conscious beings lying helter-skelter, the body pulsing, the mind gone to some other universe. The orbit around the drug. The cycle of addiction not much different than the cycle of violence.

I moved from Brooklyn to Hell's Kitchen and was living in a tiny back room in an apartment so dirty that when I touched the heavy drapes, clouds of dust wafted off and into the air. It was a dim and grimy place that looked out onto 49th Street. I was lucky to get it. It was cheap, and I could barely afford it. My landlord/roommate took the train north to the suburbs a few nights a week to be with his fiancé in their real house. So I had time alone. Otherwise, I hid awkwardly in my room while he was there. My room with the window that faced the concrete block wall on the other side of the air shaft. But I was now closer to meetings and could more easily and safely attend them.

I was terrified of these 12-step people I didn't know. Terrified of my shame. I didn't say a word. I listened to their stories. I listened to the slogans. Read them over and over. I left as soon as the meeting ended. But I kept attending meetings.

I listened to people on the Upper East Side, Chelsea, SoHo, the East Village, addicts and parents, husbands, wives, boyfriends, girlfriends.

The poor and the wealthy. I listened to people scream and wail about the abuse they suffered from alcoholic parents. I swam in the pain, the stories, the struggle to reach through the chaos to light. I hesitantly told some of my stories and left quickly after the meetings. I didn't know how to connect to these strangers or what to say beyond telling the story of my suffering and my attempts to free myself.

Stepping Stones

The 12 Step Programs use slogans to help us begin to reorganize our inner chaos. The slogans started to stick. Let Go and Let God. First Things First. HALT, Hungry, Angry, Lonely, Tired. (Let Go and Let God presents the idea that it isn't all up to me, that there is a "higher power" that can be called upon. First Things First helps to prioritize when anxiety is high. HALT means we need to address those states of being and take care of ourselves.) I used them as little tools to help me stop the swirling anxiety I was caught in. I grabbed onto them. I bought some books with daily affirmations. Anything to help my mind move out of confusion and fear and into a stillness or a temporary clarity. Anything to hold onto so I wasn't swept out into the sea of not knowing, of overwhelm and panic.

One night, my boyfriend Eric didn't show up. We were going to go out. I waited and waited. I called and called. He didn't answer his phone. What has happened to him? My mind began to turn. Freaked out, I couldn't sleep. Was he okay? Was he in danger? The slogan, Let Go and Let God, emerged in my mind. I grabbed onto it, repeated it over and over, a mantra, until some part of me knew that this situation was out of my hands. Until I could let go just a little bit.

So I could know that maybe it wasn't just up to me. So I didn't have to be the one to try and keep him safe. So, I could leave him in the hands of his angels and finally go to sleep.

Eyes Turning Inward

I explained to Eric what he needed to change so that he would be okay. Over and over. Blindly. As if he just needed to be told. As if a missing map of what to do was the problem.

But it was me who had missed a huge piece of the puzzle. Eric needed to take responsibility for his own life. He had his own choices to make, his own demons to battle. He didn't need the "help" I was trying to give him. Sure, he was happy to have me pick up all the slack he was creating in his life, but he didn't want to "face the music," so to speak.

The bad things that happened to me as a result of this relationship were severe enough that I eventually realized I had a problem and needed to deal with it if I wanted to reclaim my life. The day after I kicked him out of my apartment was the day he went to rehab (at least for the first time during our relationship).

I had and still have compassion for this person. He had lovely qualities mixed in with destructive ones. He had a difficult start in life. Maybe it wasn't his fault – but it sure wasn't mine. And I wasn't able to let him be responsible for his own life and his own choices. I stood between him and the consequence of his actions – tried to save him from his life. And who is responsible for one's life and actions but oneself?

My need had interfered. I needed him to be there for me. I fought his addiction as if it were the enemy. I fought because I wanted a real partner. I wanted the part of him that adored me, not the part of him that used crack to escape his reality. I hadn't yet separated my feelings of love from my choice to keep that love or not. I didn't know how to walk away. I didn't know you could walk away from love. My history had left me so hungry for love and un-empowered in the realm of self-care and making good choices.

You Are Not Powerless

I have repeated this destructive pattern more than once, although never as severely as in my relationship with Eric. Each time, I realized the person could not honor me; they were lost in their own reality – and I wasn't seeing the personal responsibility each of these people had for their own lives. We were looking at ghosts, filling in who we thought the other person was or should be.

I was caught in a "projection." I took my belief that there are victims who are powerless and not responsible for their own lives, and I cast this belief over somebody who could "hook" it or hold the projection. In this case, for me, an addict who appeared to be a victim. Because I saw only two classes of people – victims and perpetrators- without much complexity- I didn't initially understand how these people had created their own reality. I projected my own hurt and sense of victimhood onto them. It was as if I were trying to rescue the part of myself that had felt victimized in my own life. Except that it wasn't me. I didn't have control of their lives. And their lives were their own creative project – not mine.

This was the real beginning of my work on myself. This is when I realized that to find myself, I first had to heal myself. That I was too damaged to have a real life. That fixing this damaged self was, first and foremost, what I had to do with my life.

And so, I did.

✷

Inanna

Seeking
I descend
to my depths.
Shedding
cloaks, layers, veils
shoulds, have tos
tears, fears
the voices that cry and clutch
with bony fingers.
Shed down to my
white glistening bones
down to
the eye
that sees in the dark.

Fairy Godmother Exercise

It is 2008, and I am so stuck I cannot find a way to rescue myself. I am between marriages, and my hunger for connection means that I cannot unlatch from a man who is not what I need him to be. My friend Mikaela drives to my house to help release me from what I am caught in.

We use a fairy godmother process created by Violet Oaklander, a Gestalt therapist whose book *Windows to Our Children* enabled me to work with children in a way nobody else had.

Mikaela guides me through the exercise. We talk about how I am stuck. She asks me to draw a picture of the part of me that is caught. The part I want to release and integrate so I can free myself.

Demon Child

I draw a picture. What emerges scares me. She is a child – wild, crazy looking, desperate, screaming, ungrounded, hungry, starving to be loved, to be filled. Her eyes are X's. Her vagina gaping and hungry. Left parenthesis, explanation, right parenthesis. Loud, prominent. Tears run down her face. Her hair kinky. A wild, hungry demon child.

Mikaela asks each part of the demon child to speak. She points to the hair first, "twisted, kinky, lost," the hair says. What do your eyes have to say? "Sad, sad, sad, can't see." Your tears? "Drowning." Your heart? "Broken, broken, broken." Your vagina? "Starving, feed me, feed me." Starving to be loved, to be filled.

We talk about when this part came into being, how starved I was for love growing up.

Mikaela asks me to be the fairy godmother and talk to the hungry and lost demon child. We pick a stuffed animal to represent the child. I speak to the child. Tell her it will be okay. Feed her good thoughts, good feelings. Tell her it is not her fault she is so hungry. The adult me begins to reparent this part. Help her heal. Help her integrate.

Finally, she asks me to look at the drawing again. I am less horrified. I see her sadness instead of her deformity.

Unhooked

When we have finished, I understand how I am hooked. I see the part of me that is starved. I am not yet able to let go of this relationship that is hurting me, but clarity has descended. I have met her, the stuck one, the one who appears and takes over, the one who needs to be healed. She is why I cannot walk away. She is finally seen, identified, and given a voice. Now, I can begin to relate to her.

We often don't understand why we get stuck in situations. There is always a reason. When we are not held, told that we are loved, made to feel valued, we end up hungry or starving. That starving part of us takes over. It runs the show. Because it is emotional. What it really needs is to be fed to mature. It needs to be helped to grow up and mature so that it doesn't sabotage the rest of the personality or life.

✻

Do You?

Do you see
your radiance?
Bright like a Quasar,
the light of a trillion suns.

Do you see your size?
The universe expanding within?
The multitude of cells speaking,
in harmony with the others.

Do you see your strength?
How you can both love and stand strong?
How you can get back up
kiss the wound
forgive the wounder?

Do you see your courage?
To say yes. To say no.
To find your place and speak from it.

Do you know
you do not have to save
anybody
not even yourself?

Set your intention.
Take your steps.
Let the magic of the universe
unfold.

Compassion

In my mind's eye, I see an image of blood on the soil; the red of the blood wound soaks into and darkens the soil of the body. Soon, they are not separate. My wound was feeling unloved, heightened sensitivity, not knowing whose pain I was feeling. I misplaced compassion because it came from a wound. The blood of compassion melted into the earth of my body. I cannot tell what is what. I cannot tell where I am and where my compassion is. This image is filled with tears that I have lived, yet the ending is fruitful. I have separated the solidness of myself from the feeling of compassion. The reddish-black mud is no more. I now stand on solid ground while my red heart pumps the blood of compassion through me.

My compassion is double-sided. It includes the positive side that gives to those who need my help and the negative side that has entangled me with those who need to help themselves. Compassion has also been complicated for me because it was mixed in with my difficulty in not disappointing another. As a kid, my mother once held out her hand with four candies – one for each of us. I took the least favorite flavor. I was willing to sacrifice what I wanted so my siblings could have what they wanted. I was willing to feel disappointment, so they did not have to.

My confusion stemmed from seeing the sufferer as a victim. This is not always true. Rescuing the persecuted or underdog is one thing. Rescuing an addicted person is another. Compassion is not rescuing. It is feeling the other person's pain. It is standing beside them. Compassion does not mean you agree with how someone else sees reality.

It is understanding, caring, and respecting their reality – because that is the place they live.

What was missing in me was the ability to tolerate the lesson needed, that sometimes the seemingly wounded, while not responsible for their wounds, must be accountable for the part they played. That compassion is not a buffer but a support.

Yet my compassion was slanted. I didn't have compassion for those I saw as responsible for the pain of innocent others or sometimes for those who caused my own pain. It was as if I lived in a black-and-white universe. There were those who were victims and those who were perpetrators. I still, at times, struggle with this. Perhaps the complexity of my father left me with this view. He could be mean and cause hurt, yet he contained worlds of his own hurt. Sometimes, I could see his pain. Other times, all I could see was a raging bully. Somehow, I got split into two people with two lenses. Somehow, I had two dads. The good one and the bad one. I didn't see this split until my mid-twenties, nor did I integrate these parts of him into one person until much later.

Rescuer

I am a rescuer of the hurt. I speak for those who cannot speak for themselves. I have always had empathy for those people, animals, and even plants that were struggling, abused, or in pain. I felt their pain.

Since I was small, I have rescued and brought home hurt and baby birds, abandoned cats, and dogs. The baby birds fallen out of the nest.

The kittens dumped in the middle of nowhere with a short life of starvation ahead of them. The wild dog that our dogs attacked one snowy winter that my father left to its fate. I nursed sick animals. My compassion helped me. It brought my animal friends nearer to me. I opened my being to them, I doled out love. I cared for them and, in doing so, felt cared for by them. This was life-saving for me. It meant I was part of a flow of love, of nurturing, of caring. It meant I felt loved. It also meant that I could make the world safer for others, which meant I was making the world safer for me.

Wild Dog

I am a teenager. It is winter. A cold Pennsylvania winter. When my father came back from his daily mile walk to the mailbox and casually mentioned our dogs had attacked another dog, I put on my coat and walked down the road, looked for footprints in the snow veering, off into the woods. Half a mile down, I saw the dark impressions in fresh white snow, little for Shaver and large for Bruno, and another set mixed in with theirs. I followed the footprints to the creek. Lying in the icy bright water, paralyzed – most likely with cold, was a little wild dog. He tried to bite me when I attempted to pick him up. I managed to lift his immobile body out of the freezing water. I took off my coat, carefully wrapped him in it, and began the long walk home, my arms feeling as if they would fall off and keeping his face away from me so I wouldn't get bitten. When I got home, I put him in the kitchen which was warm, and he hid behind the coal stove. He stayed there for a few days until my father chased him out of the house, back into the winter. Although he claimed it was an accident and that the dog ran outside when he opened the door, I knew that was not true.

My father was concerned with his own comfort, not the comfort of others. He saw the dog as a hindrance, an interruption that was not part of his plan. He saw the interruption, not the opportunity, in that situation. The opportunity to care, to see who I was, to see my caring soul. He could have bonded with me over my caring for others. He could have said, "Sometimes we have to interrupt what we think we want, our plan to instead take care of those around us." He did not. He did not see my need to assist that lost dog. He did not see my pain.

There is a lesson here. The lesson to go with what is instead of swimming upstream against it, pushing it aside, pretending it does not exist. We are at times, asked to open and see more than our narrow path, our ambition, what we think we want. We are sometimes asked to remove our blinders and join the others who have entered our lives.

Unconscious

I am still healing, still on this journey, and despite my growth, I sometimes feel revulsion or disgust. There are injuries people cause that I have not found a way to forgive. When somebody intentionally hurts someone else, human or animal, I have difficulty seeing their brokenness with empathy. I struggle to see their fear, their unconsciousness. I have seen pictures of abused animals that stopped me cold and left images imprinted in me that I have not been able to fully push away. The unconsciousness that can see another as an object and not feel their value terrifies me. For me to find my compassion here would open worlds of grief. It seems better for me to push away these unconscious others with hatred and anger. But is it? My grief is real.

My grief that the world can be so cold. My grief that I am part of a world where we do not honor each other. My grief for the pain the injured being has suffered.

Closer Look

I know there is a wall of rage in that person, and under it, enormous grief. Regardless, it is their actions that we see and use to evaluate a person. And if those actions have hurt someone else, then I am in quandary. Whose pain do I side with? The one who hurts or the hurt?

Historically, I have always sided with the one obviously hurt. And yet, I have a need to look closer.

Haven't we all been both? Don't we switch those roles easily? I don't hurt people on purpose, but looking back through my history, I have undoubtedly hurt others. Yet, I see myself as someone who doesn't harm others. Many of us see ourselves that way. And we all have experienced pain. Claiming both sides of ourselves, hurt and hurter allows us to stand in a larger place and to see with deeper eyes.

Gravity

We've played both parts. But the gravitational pull of knowing draws me to the one who was burned, not the one who burned. It pulls me to understanding pain and trauma far more than understanding the blaming and hatred. It pulls me to align with the inner knowing of spirit and away from structured hierarchical belief. Towards spirituality, away from religion. I take my compassion with me and shy away from predetermined boxes.

Sometimes, when we have compassion, when we feel another's pain intensely, we want to scoop them up and rescue them. We don't want to see them in pain or experience their pain ourselves. Rescuing others is precious – especially if it is an innocent animal or child. However, it is not so great when it blocks the person from taking responsibility or tackling an aspect of his or her life.

Eyes of Truth

Now, when I feel the urge to "rescue" someone, I ask, what is his or her lesson? What is their life trying to get them to see or do? What am I putting on them that isn't the truest way of seeing this situation? Do I see them as powerless or needing help they cannot give themselves? Why can't I say no? What am I afraid of? Am I afraid of being the denying bad one? Can I stand up to their vision of reality and say, "No, I do not see it this way; I do not believe that you are a victim," while also saying, "Yes, I do have empathy for you. You are doing the best you know how, and sometimes the path of learning is tough."

✹

Co-Create

Co - to act together.
Create - to bring into being.

A lump of clay. Wet, unformed.
My hands move, push, pinch, squeeze, and pull.
The clay takes form.

Who moves my hands?
Who inspires, breathes spirit into the form?
I am not acting alone.
I do not know what is becoming.

My hands follow an unseen guidance.
This is a meditation.

My hands and the breath of spirit join.
A form emerges. A being. An expression.

I do not create alone.

Dad's World

I am sitting in my father's studio in rural PA. I am maybe twelve. The walls are dark wood. His studio is crowded; there are sculptures and paintings everywhere. My father is sitting at his easel working on a Sci-Fi illustration. He washes dark and light colors across the surface of the Masonite board. Slowly, as he paints, he brings form to these undefined masses. Cities emerge. Little highlights appear on tiny figures marching off into the landscape. Sky envelopes the scene. Atmosphere and space develop. The colors are beautiful. I am enthralled. I see how he creates scenes and stories out of tubes of color. He is patient and painstaking with his work. He is a creator god, and I learn from him that we can create something from nothing. I learn that every square inch of the painting matters and relates to every other square inch. Just like life. Every moment counts.

As a child and teenager, I enjoyed sitting with my father when he was painting in his studio. I loved to watch him paint and revel in our conversations. It was where I could enter his world and be part of it with him.

While my father was successful with his commercial work, he received little recognition for his fine art. The pieces collected in the studio, barn, and house. Yet he got up every day, went out to his studio, and worked.

My father struggled. I watched his depression ebb and flow through the years. I witnessed his internal battle with not being validated by the world. I experienced his anger and frustration as he struggled with being unseen. I remember telling him once that he was valuable whether the world saw him or not.

I so wanted him to know that he was okay. I so wanted him to be at peace. I hated watching him struggle. I was trapped in his struggle with him. I needed him to be free so I could be free. I needed him to be available in a different way. I needed him to support me instead of me supporting him.

As he became older, he began to make peace with his life. He once told me that he couldn't get up and work every day if he didn't have faith. He eventually made peace with all of his life as he was dying. I was happy he made peace with his life, but part of me wished he had regretted that he hadn't valued us more when we were growing up.

My Decision

Out of this history, I made a decision. I will not do what my father did. I will engage with the outer world. I will "make" things happen. And I did. In a sense, I moved to the opposite end of the spectrum – to try to make things happen rather than not. Just the other end of the same way of seeing things.

Recently, as my work has grown and spread out into the world, I've run into some emotional snags. I have always been somebody with a lot of will. I decide what I want to accomplish, and I make it happen. But I have always had to work hard to make things happen. Nothing has come effortlessly or even easily. I have mostly felt alone in this process.

At times, I have gotten stuck. I push, but I cannot make what I want to come into being. Emotionally, I feel as if I am falling in on myself. My world gets dark. I feel trapped and alone. I push harder. It doesn't work. I get upset. I turn into a big ball of frustration. I stop, re-evaluate, and look at myself.

I was meditating on this struggle one day. What is this? Why am I going through this? What am I doing? Why won't life cooperate with my intention right now?

This struggle is hard-wired into me. Memories emerge of myself as a child, teenager, and young adult when there was no support or help. When I was trying to do something and nobody was able or willing to help me do it or even support me emotionally in the process.

The Scar

When I was working on my portfolio to apply to art school, I could not get my father to help me, to teach me how to paint. He was too involved in his own work. Eventually, after a summer of struggle, he decided to look at what I was doing and spent some time teaching me the basics of painting.

I have a scar, jagged, rough – a part of me still gets caught in those feelings and struggles reflected in my relationship with my parents. Of needing help and my need being diminished, pushed aside, made invisible. I feel sad for my little self who tried so hard, for that part of me has always tried and tried with little support. That little self has felt very alone and still falls into feeling alone. It doesn't understand how things work. It doesn't know how to make things happen. It is the feeling I felt as a kid when I had no way out, when life hadn't yet offered me an exit plan or path into the future. When both my parents were struggling with depression and frustration. My mother overwhelmed and sometimes exploding from working full-time, raising four children, and managing many household tasks. There was very little left for us.

The Dust Settles

I've come to realize that I've outgrown the parts of me that resonate with this way of seeing. I've come to see how I ended up in a way of experiencing that is not true and will not help me continue moving forward in my life. That my arms and legs work now, that I can walk and move, that I am no longer crippled. I have to remind myself that I can change how I see things, that there are other vistas, other ways to perceive.

Some aspects of my life are much bigger than me and out of my control. Like the years when we were waiting for our house to sell so we could move. How my business and work progress. My health. My husband's health. In the moment, concerns about these things can crowd out how good my life is – I have a great place to live, creative freedom, a wonderful loving relationship with my husband, and I am doing work I love. And yet, an inner battle still gets activated. Like walking through a dry dirt path, just the process of walking through causes dust to get kicked up. As I continue, all that is still unresolved in myself gets stirred up and swirls about. I accept this as part of the process of life, and yet, I also intend to resolve this current batch of dust and move on, less encumbered.

What is this dust? Why do I fall into these moments of feeling trapped? Ancient and familiar. What is under this? Fear? It is fear. I am afraid. I don't understand the interplay of magic and my task. I don't understand that I will organically be led to what I must focus on next, the next step of my becoming.

Is there really magic, flow, alignment? Can I trust it? How do I manifest without pushing so hard? What can I trust?

Where is my role? What if I stay stuck? What if I didn't do enough? How do I know? This is the knot I get caught in. It is as if I do not understand what creation is and my role in it. All of this is fear. I am afraid. I am scared. I am no longer in control. As vast parts of my life sit, seemingly undone, perhaps at another level, they are growing, waiting, brewing.

I go back to my dad and his struggle. Dad couldn't get his fine art out into the world. I lived with that. I suffered as I watched him suffer. I loved him and wanted him to be happy.

What if the world doesn't want my offerings either? Perhaps that is what is driving my desperation. So, who do I turn into? I turn into an upset person trying to make it happen all by myself.

Co-Creation

There is a new and other place for me to stand. It is in the realm of trust and magic. It is in the knowing that I can open up a new space for myself to live out of – a space with more room, more grace, and more beauty. A space where the universe cooperates with my desires. Where it is a co-creation. I lean into a trust of what is, what is becoming. I release my timetable. My desire that what I want needs to manifest now. So much is out of my hands. There is no way I can do it alone.

Before, whenever something didn't happen or was delayed, I felt as if I had to do it myself and that moving forward was being blocked. If I am the world, if I am part of the god-force, the light, the breath of spirit, then this will happen. If I am the small self, I am stuck because I cannot do it. It is too big of a job for me alone.

I am more than my small self. I claim my larger self, the self that connects to the universe. I claim that I can co-create. I am no longer encumbered and trapped. I stop seeing myself as alone, pushing uphill. I call in a new vision. I ask for ease and grace. I ask that I enjoy each moment. I let go of the outcome and claim the beauty of the journey.

Singing Into Our Bones

There is a piece of magic here. It is the magic of believing that it is not all up to me. Instead, I co-create and co-participate. It is the magic of believing that the universe is ultimately friendly if I engage in it in the right way. It is the magic of trusting that it is not all up to me. If my work is meant to expand outward, then it will. We live in a magical and psychological universe. A hologram. A web of interconnection and synchronicities. Every experience, every step I take is whole. It unfolds as it does, in part because of who I am. As I attend to and tackle my inner obstacles and demons, the outer world smooths out as well.

This is the new choice for me. It is a truer choice. It is not all up to me. It is a choice that allows for a more encompassing understanding of our world. It is a choice that knows magic is possible and co-participates with it. It is a choice that shows me that I am not alone. This perspective is essential for me to step out into the bigger world. When we sing into our bones, breathe strength and life into them, and make ourselves whole, the path opens. This is the underpinning of this new world and my new world.

5
Releasing The Binds

But most important of all, she explained that it was all right to say 'No. I disagree.' That was a gift. I understood it was power. The power to think my own thoughts. The power to believe in myself.
~ Alice Hoffman

Fire of Divinity

There is much work needed if we are to find our true selves, our inner voice, the parts of us that did not develop or were suppressed. For we carry cloaked around us other's voices, needs, desires. We carry the judgment of others, our cultures, the patriarchal voice that denies inner knowing, and the feminine aspects of the divine. We carry rules and ideas that suppress our connection to our intuition. We carry also imprints from other lifetimes. Instead of walking in the cool wind of inner knowing, we cling to what feels safe, what we understand, what we have been taught. Life, however, offers us opportunities to grow. To cast off these layers. To leave behind ways of being that do not serve us.

As we walk deeper into the fire of our divinity, we release the binds constricting us, separating us from ourselves.

We descend, looking for our bones so that we may grow new and more authentic flesh.

Inanna, the Sumerian goddess known as the "Queen of Heaven," descended to the underworld, where her sister Ereshkigal turned her into a corpse. She later rises from the dead and returns to heaven. In the descent, she sheds the layers of her former self, confronts her shadow, and later returns reborn -an integrated being. Like Inanna's descent to the underworld and her return, we may choose or be forced to journey into the underworld to re-experience our shadow, recovering the parts of ourselves that were lost. In doing so, we learn to hear the voice of our intuition and find our authority.

Layers

Releasing the binds includes healing. It includes learning to say no. It includes being dragged down into the underworld until we gain clarity and remove what has cloaked us. It includes rebuilding the self and bringing back parts not fully formed or lost to trauma. As a person who could not say no, as I found myself in compromised situations, I began to see. I began to look at what I wanted, not look at what would make you keep me, love me, like me, accept me. I began to find my own feet instead of needing to please you. The people pleaser had to go away. She had to be removed, healed, lifted up, and out of her box.

My path included many ways. One of them was therapy.

Therapy is a descent, both conscious and temporary. I began the dive down into talking about what I had lived through.

What my past had made me into. How I was dis-empowered.

Where I was weak, riddled with the stink of shame, and frightened.

I remember looking with fear at one of my therapists. She seemed so large, so powerful. I was afraid to disappoint her. I wanted to leave therapy at one point. She told me I wasn't ready. I listened. Not because I was sure she was right but because I could not yet say no. That alone was telling. I was not ready to leave, if only for that reason.

I have had to drop the expectations put on me, shed them layer by layer to find myself and my value. We unwrap ourselves from the binds of our history. Releasing the binds means removing the bondages placed on us or that we were born into. It means I take what is yours and give it back to you. What you expect of me is not mine. I will not hold it for you.

Walking Away

Once our structure is more solid, we can remove what we no longer need. Your expectations or approval. Your desires or hopes. We must be conscious to do this. Removing is often simply rising above. Sometimes, it is moving out of shame and into anger. Other times, it is moving out of anger and into acceptance. Regardless, we may have to say that what happened is what was. It is not who I am now. Or we may have to say, no, your behavior is not good enough. And simply walk away, whether literally or internally.

Vessel

When we develop that power, when we are standing on our own feet and have released ourselves from the restrictions that we and others have placed on us, from perspectives that cloud us, then what comes through us is authentically ours. Then, our abilities shine with clarity. We become clearer vessels for the divine.

MAVERICK

I am not a soft wooly sheep.
Not in an enclosure, hemmed in.
I do not follow
Your fences.

I find my own truths.
My thoughts freely wander.
My mind a bird in the sky
Beyond horizons.

I do not conform
Fit myself into your desires.
I do not take your word
Over my own.

I have the ability to choose.

Take your own strong hand
Grab onto it.
It is yours.

When Love Isn't Enough

A year before my marriage to my second husband, one of my best friends walked out of our friendship. To have stopped her would have cost me too much.

Years after our breakup, years after I had finally moved on, Alice sent me a Facebook message. I read it in shock. I wasn't expecting it. I had let go and moved on a long time ago. She wanted to know if I would consider reconnecting. She let me know she kept a picture of the two of us on her dresser. As I read it, a strong No formed in my body.

I wrote her a letter. Much shorter than what follows.

NO

No. I felt a hard stone form in my gut. No. I will not.
That dance has ended.
Your beauty is still there. I see it.
But I am done.

No. Finally, my feet have ground.
Strong. Firm.
I do not diminish you.
My roots reach deep, deeper.
My branches sway in the sky.

No.
You are released.
I am free.

Letter for Alice

Thank you for reaching out and letting me know you are doing well. I appreciate your apology.

When I read your message, pain erupted through me. What happened between us in the past was heartbreaking for me. It has been eight years since we have had contact. After we split, it took me months to find myself again. My mind turning over and over. My heart broken. Trying to understand. Where did our love go? What happened? My sense of loss was overwhelming.

Fissure

How had this chapter started? The chapter of my blindness, descent, and ultimate return? Maybe when I saw you competing with other women? I didn't understand why you flirted with their husbands and boyfriends. I didn't understand why you felt these women were threatened by you. I was puzzled, but I accepted your feelings.

I saw what I loved. I did not see the cracks in our characters that would split open; the end already written years before the break. I did not see how my love for you blinded me to your weaknesses or how you could not take accountability for your actions. This "love" with its flaws organically built into each of us inevitably would crash.

Close Friend

You had been my close friend. We would talk deep into the night, intellectually well-matched and finding new worlds in the depth psychology. We used to stay up for hours at night, discussing healing.

Our mental connection was wondrous. The forays into the thoughts of Carl Jung, Freud, and Winnicott. Richard Tarnas and Stan Groff. Lionel Corbett. The ideas of healing and holding, descent and ascent, the collective unconscious. An excitement generated between us.

Lure

You were sober then. But a few years later, you began questioning your sobriety. You talked about wanting to have a drink on occasion. Somehow, I didn't see you falling off the wagon. I was naive. I believed you would be okay. And it seemed you were for a while – at least on the outside.

I didn't see your inner angst. I didn't see your dissatisfaction. I didn't see you trying to fill the needs of your spirit with the mundane.

Several years later, after you told me about walking out into the ocean and not wanting to turn around and come back, I realized you were suicidal. I didn't know why you were struggling.

I didn't know what your job entailed, how it was soul-sucking and required dishonesty and manipulation, how it was impacting your soul, or that money and fun were your gods then.

I didn't know why your employment ended or how you lost your condo. I didn't know about the cocaine, the party life you had been living. I didn't realize all these disasters were coming out of a life being mismanaged, abused. Inner demons that had their hold on you.

A spirit being cannot thrive in a life built around the superficial.

Confusion

Divorcing and living alone, I invited you to live with me for a while so you could get back on your feet. I saw the part of you that was spiritual, the part that loved animals. I saw the part that was intelligent and deep.

We lived together for a while. You were a support to me while also struggling. Drinking heavily. Looking for men.

Eventually, you moved further away, seeking work. We maintained our connection. I visited you, but weird things began to occur: stories, behaviors, events. They snuck up slowly. Nothing so big that I saw a warning.

It was more like the wind getting incrementally stronger until you realize the trees are wildly swaying and you are in the middle of a storm.

What to Say?

Your behavior was confusing to me and, at times, not okay. There was the time you said to me about my second husband-to-be, "I could have had him." What did you mean? Did you mean he would have picked you over me had you wanted him? Did you mean that you were more special than I?

Were you jealous of me? Regardless, that sentence dropped like a stone to the pit of my stomach. I didn't say anything at the time. I didn't know what to say.

I want you to know you could not have had him. He did not want you. My relationship with this man was not about your will or your ability to manipulate. It was not about your delusion that you were sexier than I. This was not about "catching" a man. This was about a deep love between me and another being, which we have nurtured and enabled to bloom.

Pedestal

I admired you, looked up to you. I was more grounded. You were more psychic. And you were more sophisticated than I.

More versed in style and fashion, you helped me "spruce up" after my divorce. But underneath, you still had an addiction, the person who had stopped using cocaine years before but hadn't rooted out her desire for the sensation of bliss, and I was, to some degree, still an enabler and caretaker, a person whose heart did not yet have enough boundaries. I was still manipulatable.

Our split started with me crossing one of my own boundaries.

Your Lie

After you hit bottom, after the loss of everything you had, after the rehab, after you moved across the country and then came back, I believed you when you told me you were clean, that you had stopped drinking, that you wanted to get back into 12-Step work with your old sponsor.

I never imagined that you would begin drinking again, that you would talk about AA as if it were the enemy.

You were temporarily staying with my husband and me while looking for a place to live. We were trying to help you transition. We wanted to support your new sobriety. We believed you were committed to your health. I suggested you find a room in a house where there would be no credit check.

Not good enough for you. You wanted an apartment and said your mother would co-sign. You found an apartment. Then, at the last minute, you told me your mother could not co-sign a lease because she was out of state. Would I help you?

Riptide

I wanted to say no. My gut screamed for me to say no. I could not. I could not honor my feelings. I could not find a way to say no. Instead, I tried to set it up so things would be okay. I tried to manipulate the outer world rather than listen to my inner voice. I allowed you to convince me to co-sign your lease. In that moment, I betrayed myself and my inner knowing.

Why didn't I think to myself - you created this? But I didn't. I, who always looks at the best of a person, saw that you were trying to put your life back together. I just wasn't looking at me; what had grabbed me, the descent I would be pulled into. I didn't see myself, my need to be involved, my deep-seated distrust of allowing a person and their problems to work out in their own way, with the universe, without me.

When it was time to sign, you had it arranged; I would be signing the lease, not both of us. A surprise. A red flag.

And my own red flag, that I continued forward, that I could not say no and walk away. The lure of being needed, of helping, and the deception you maneuvered that you were pulling your life back together – those combined were too strong. A riptide I could not free myself from.

My Word

The lease was month to month. I set it up so that I was protected. I insisted that I hold a month of security deposit in addition to the month the landlady held. That way, nobody would get hurt. The security deposit would go to me first, not you. I foresaw no problems. More than safe, I thought.

Shortly after you moved in, you began to complain about your sponsor, the woman who had helped you years before, the woman you had moved back here to work with again. Then you quit Alcoholics Anonymous and began drinking again. You were out at night prowling around, ready for an argument, breaking rules, acting belligerent. Neighbors were complaining. You eventually burned your local bridges and decided to relocate.

The fleas left behind by your cats severely bit the next tenant. Several times. Until multiple flea bomb sessions finally killed them all. You wanted your security deposit back right away. All of it.

You didn't want to take responsibility for the damage you left behind. You had a nasty interaction with the landlady. But it was my lease. It was my signature. It was my word. I would not tarnish my word any more than I already had. I backed up the landlady. No money back until the fleas were gone and any damage was fixed.

I dealt with the upset landlady and used the security deposit to pay for damages. You were furious and couldn't believe I chose to honor my word instead of taking care of you. You wanted that money and had no interest in making things right. I apologized to the landlady. It was embarrassing, humbling to see how I had fallen into co-dependency with someone who had been teetering and was now entirely out of control.

How did I fall so far off track? How did you sway me so? Your addiction was ugly; it twisted you, and I did not fully comprehend it. I saw the beauty of your soul, and I loved you.

A Line

There was no way I was backing down. I hadn't signed up for this. What you had done wasn't okay. Lying. Expecting others to take care of your problems. Not owning up to your behavior. Not honoring your agreements. I wrote you a letter telling you my feelings.

I needed you to step up and talk about what happened between us. I told you that we had to talk. That we needed to work out what had happened.

You refused to talk. "No, I am not going to discuss this. Let's take a break," you said.

No. I will not. I will not take a break. Friends work through the hard stuff. They hash through, explore, discuss. They don't sweep differences under the rug. I tell you that I am unwilling to sweep things under the rug, that we need to talk, or it is over. You refuse to talk, and so it ends.

No. I will not. I will not take a break. Friends work through the hard stuff. They hash through, explore, discuss. They don't sweep differences under the rug. I tell you that I am unwilling to sweep things under the rug, that we need to talk, or it is over. You refuse to talk and so it ends.

Your Refusal

You walked away. You had no intention of looking inside or being accountable. I had no intention of being there for someone who could not look at themselves or work out a real relationship.

What had just happened? One of my best friends. I am dazed, confused. I hurt, hurt, hurt.

There was no way around it. There was nothing I could do because the block in you had nothing to do with me. It was a block you had in yourself. There was a part of yourself you were hiding from. For you to open up and look at yourself, at your underlying shame and wounding, would have caused you to have to let go of your entire identity. You couldn't look at yourself, and I could no longer have that kind of relationship.

I can finally see. I do not back down.

※

A Voice

One morning, out of the blue, after a night of tossing and turning, wondering, trying to understand what had happened, I heard a voice in my head, distinct, strong.

"She cannot honor you." Crystal clear. No negotiating. No wiggle room. Simple.

The voice, those words – a gift from spirit. That message rang through me with a clarity that woke me up, turned me around. That message allowed me to deeply sigh, to release the breath I had been holding. That message helped me release my sense of guilt, my self-blame. It helped release me from the nightly tossing and turning, the wondering and doubting. The confusion that our relationship was not strong enough for you to step up fully. That is when the confusion cleared, and I began to fully let go.

Caring

I still care about her, but I am not willing to be in contact with someone who cannot honor me. I am here to learn to love myself.

I think of Alice when she was staying with me after my divorce. We slept in the same bed, my huge king-size bed. I remember hearing her breathe, feeling her presence near me. It made me feel safe to have someone with me. I was still traumatized from my divorce. I needed friends around me. And she was that.

The Physical

We are physical beings, and a physical presence can be soothing and calming. We attach to the presence of others, the touch of their bodies, or the sound of their voice. Imagine being a child. We are held and rocked. We are bathed and dressed. We are fed and cuddled. Yet, if it turns out that a parent gets mad at us or uses us in some way, it is confusing. We need them, even when they are not fully there for us. This creates a conflict, a struggle. We love, and yet the person we love is not honoring us. This has been my struggle. To walk away from someone who isn't honoring me, even though I am "attached," love them, and feel that I need them.

A Kind of Love

Alice and I each had our weaknesses. She wanted me to give more, to allow more. I had already given her too much. She saw me as second to her. Less valuable. Like Robin to her Batman. I was there for her, but we were not equals in her eyes. Yet we loved each other.

Mythical Bird

Red, blue, green, yellow
aplomb with brilliant feathers

You explode into flames
diminish into ash,
a small pile.

Reborn,
the end, only the beginning.

The Phoenix

Alice once had a spiritual session and was given the image of the phoenix rising. The phoenix is an immortal bird that cyclically regenerates or is reborn. It dies in a fire of its own making and burns into a pile of ash. Rising from the ashes of its predecessor, the newly reborn phoenix regains life and is, in that way, immortal. Rebirth after the destruction of the outer life. The inner life enriched from the previous experiences.

Alice had her own lessons. She had damaged her life. She wouldn't like to hear that. In her mind, I believe she thought it had just happened, at least at the time. That she had been a victim, not a player in the game. Perhaps she has not yet fully risen from the ashes of what was. Perhaps she is rising, reborn, or at least in the process. I hope so.

The phoenix also applies to me. I, too, have crashed and burned. I, too, have damaged my life and found myself rising from the ashes, newly formed. The fiery feathers grown back in, brilliant reds and blues, greens, and yellows, ready again to fly.

Clarity

I looked within. Why had I had this experience? Where was I culpable?

I looked at how this person I thought was my dear and close friend could have done this, not just to her own life, to the landlady, but to me. The dynamic became clear.

The part of me that struggled saying no, that was a caretaker of others – thinking that the person needed help instead of seeing the teaching that life was trying to give them.

I learned something from that. It was a lesson I had learned before but one I had to learn again. The power of addiction snuffs out love. And love Alice, I did. I had helped her time and time again. Out of love. Then, the love I had for her was stronger than the love I had for myself.

On My Feet

I've changed a lot in these past eight years. I no longer need or desire a connection with Alice. I have no interest in being pulled in again. I no longer wish to be friends with people who shed their inappropriate behavior on others with no regard. I do not wish to be in a co-dependent relationship – which clearly was the case for me. And I have found my value. I see my strength, my brightness, and beauty.

You say you are sober and on a joyous path. I am happy for you. But so much of what happened was not and is still not okay for me – and still feels ugly. I do not know what you have and have not resolved in your life. I do not know where your beliefs are still crooked and self-serving. I have been left with no trust in you.

I am not the person I used to be. We would not fit together the same way, perhaps not fit at all. I am glad to be free, to be entirely on my feet, and to have found my wholeness and completeness. May you also find your healing, your power, what you have been seeking.

✹

Have I Told You?

Have I told you? That it wasn't okay.
That your best wasn't good enough.
That you were not your best.

Have I told you? That I am worthy. That I deserve.
That I am a small sun and glowing.

Have I told you? That I see myself. That I hold myself.
That I reject your treatment of me.

Have I told you? That I would become more.
That I have. That one can outgrow another.

Have I told you? Of my beautiful life.
My life that came from me. That with each step away,
I grew stronger.

Have I told you? You were only a chapter.
A chapter completed. A memory washed away.

Divorce

When I was fifty-two, I woke up and realized that I was angry with my ex-husband – five years after our divorce. I'd been remarried just over a month – in a marriage with someone I adore, someone I don't have to fight to be close to. Because I am in my future, and out of the confusion of that time, I can look back more easily and sort through what occurred. I haven't told anybody the full truth of what happened during my divorce. It was too much to speak. Some of it too ugly. I could not get the story out of my mouth, the pain out of my body. Nor did many people know of the many difficult moments of my marriage. Today, I'm angry enough to see my truth and to tell it. And so, just as I wrote about my relationship with Alice, I write this story, sharing my voice with the world.

Path of Learning

What is a relationship? What is love? What does it mean when love is a path of learning and growth but not the nourishing food, we all wish it to be? We supposedly loved each other. You supposedly loved me.

I knew when it was over. I felt the click as that knowing fell into place. I still needed to spend a month or more getting ready to tell you, trying to find a place to stand, making sure I could trust my knowing. I had a crush on someone else. Just a crush, no more. Simply because he could look straight into my eyes. Something you stopped doing, something you had avoided for a long time.

It was okay when I first told you I was finished. You were apologetic. You knew you hadn't been there. Perhaps you were still hoping I would change my mind.

Yet when things weren't going how you wished, everything changed. You got mean, sharp darts of hate coming out of your eyes. The way you looked at me.

Did your disappointment and hurt make you hate? Did hating me make it easier for you? I didn't hate you. But I am angry. I'm angry because I didn't deserve to be treated that way. I'm angry at who you let yourself be. At the choices you made, the choice to hate instead of love. I thought you were a better person.

Wounded

Cunt. Bitch. Those words lodged into my body, slowly seeping their shadowy poison. As if I was suddenly a different person than the person you said you loved, who you said you wanted to stay and work it out with.

But I wouldn't and couldn't stay, and you began to punish and abuse me. It wasn't the same kind of punishment that occurred in our marriage. Then, when you felt your shame or some other uncomfortable feeling, you pushed me away with your anger and criticism, with your neglect. That was mild compared to what you turned into. You threatened me. You treated me as if you hated me. Who said that just because you were mad, you could treat me like that? Who said that you had the right? You did not. You trampled on me because it was the only way you could deal with your feelings about the events of your life. You trampled on me instead of looking at yourself. Maybe you were that person all along. I didn't see it. I never imagined it would go that way.

"I have to hold it together," I think to myself. "I have to be careful." I already feel as if I could die, as if I won't survive this hatred coming at me.

I hold myself in tight. I make myself small. "Don't move. Don't make a sound," I tell myself.

I didn't know if I had the right to protect myself. I felt guilty that you were struggling with my leaving and guilty that I was leaving. I needed to get through the mediation without the whole thing blowing up. I didn't want a legal battle. I took on your negative energy. I couldn't block your hatred from entering my body, ricocheting and piercing. My physical body started to deteriorate. I became emaciated, down fifteen pounds from my already small size, my hair falling out in hunks, my period dried up and gone away. My digestion stopped working right, and my stomach bloated and enlarged – as if I were pregnant. "I have to get through this," my new mantra. I could not imagine the fire in our lives getting any bigger. I could not imagine managing or surviving a full-scale war. There was no room for me to be angry. I was too afraid. How do you confront someone's mistreatment of you when you are wounded, terrified, and unsafe?

How does this happen, the bullying of another being? How does the heart close so firmly and with such hatred? How does it darken and harden?

You made our parting miserable, painful, destructive. I ask myself, whom did I fall in love with? With whom did I try to "make it work" all those years? Who are you? Where did your goodness go? Was it only selective – if I pleased you, then you loved me, but if I did not, you turned? I deserved better than that. You deserved better than allowing yourself to go there. We all deserve better than that.

Worlds Apart

I loved our house. The house I found. The house we both put so much into. The house in the trees that made me feel as if I lived in a world that was beautiful and special – away from the hustle and bustle of city life. It was up the canyon and allowed me to daily drive past huge jutting rocks and California brush. The drive I loved. The drive you resented and complained about constantly.

You hated living in our unfinished house, a fixer house. You hated your commute. Later, you decided you wanted to live in a loft downtown. After our divorce, you did just that. And then you moved back to our neighborhood.

'We don't have to fix it now,' I would say. There is no pressure. But there was. An earthquake I didn't anticipate was coming.

As we were divorcing, I was willing to not decide what to do with the house, to let it be something we owned together, and figure out what to do about it later. You weren't willing to do that. You had to finish everything right now. No shades of gray but black and white. No collaboration.

Our Agreement

We made an agreement. I bought the house – paid you for your share. We figured out its value and applied credits for assets I would not receive. And after I borrowed the rest and paid you, and it was in my name, then you changed your mind. You threatened me. You wanted more, me to pay you more. You refused to leave. I knew if I left, I would never keep the house I now owned.

So, I stayed and took the punishment, moving onto a mattress in the adjoining room, separated only by a sheet of plastic where a wall would eventually be.

You stopped working for the two short years I would receive the alimony I needed to build my business and become self-supporting. So, you could pay less.

Didn't you want the best for me? Didn't you want me to build my business and succeed? Be able to fully support myself? I wanted the best for you. I wanted you to grow and develop. I wanted your career to take off. I never wished you anything other than complete success.

Did your caustic bitterness consume all of you? Was there even a molecule of kindness left? I am angry for how low you stooped. You could not look at your humiliation and deal with your own feelings. Instead, you trashed me. I never saw your relatives or friends again. I was blacklisted as if I were evil.

Our divorce made me struggle with my own sense of value. Perhaps what you thought was true. Was I wrong to leave? I had so much guilt put on me. Family members who were mad and blamed me or who wanted me to stay. But they did not know what I had lived with and through.

✹

Sorting

I am on the phone with my mother. She says, "Maybe you can get back together. Maybe it isn't too late." My heart sinks. I so need support. I begin to cry. I try to explain that it is too late. I tell her that I have tried too hard for too long. "Mom," I cry, "I cannot do this anymore." She does not budge. She cannot take in my suffering. She does not comfort me. She can only see the disgrace of divorce.

Why is a divorce worse than the pain of staying in a dead marriage? And once you turned, it was too late anyway.

Perhaps I didn't deserve my half of what was ours, of what we created together. I knew what I put into our marriage was a lot. You put in more income. But I put in more love, more laundry, and shopping. I put in the effort to get us to therapy. I put in the desire for closeness. I kept asking you to show up until I gave up. I was the one who demanded that you step up and be an emotional partner – to learn to deal with that part of yourself.

Did you think our connection would take care of itself all on its own? And then you reduced it all down to money. You implied that I wasn't worth as much as you. That you helped me more than I helped you. Didn't we both put in our time and our souls? I had my heart and soul in this thing we called our marriage. Asking to end it was one of the hardest things I have done. You made it about money – that I didn't deserve anything. That splitting what we created together equally was not fair. I disagreed. I did my best to stand my ground.

Our blood, sweat, and tears were in this marriage. Our hearts. Our failures and histories.

Not just money. I toiled, too. I contributed, too. I helped you, too. You flatlined the whole thing. It wasn't really about money. It was about your shame. You failed – if you choose to look at it that way. That wasn't how I looked at it. I needed someone who wanted to look in my eyes. I needed someone who wanted to talk and cuddle. I needed someone who wanted to be *with* me.

Stories

You thought providing was enough. You felt like you made sacrifices for us. What you put in, you did of your own free will. It was never what I asked for. I would never have traded my life for security, nor would I ask you to do that. I came here for more. I came here to find myself. I came here to learn and grow. I came here to find my wings while living on earth. I asked for emotional connection. I wanted tender touch. I wanted you to want to be with me.

We no longer fit each other. We never fit. I just didn't see it. You twisted and turned it into a different story. In your story, I used you and threw you away. Not my story. I fought for us for years.

I wanted to hold onto what I felt was partly mine. I wanted to hold onto the house. The only thing that wasn't split evenly was the two years of alimony. It wasn't a lot. It was enough to give me the time to become self-sufficient. I worked hard. I did it. But I kept questioning myself. Was I being greedy? Was I being unfair? (Later, after I sold the house, the money you received, promised under duress, paid you back for the alimony you had given me. So, it was fifty-fifty after all.)

What is under my fear of being unfair? I want to be kind. I want to be considerate. I want to be ethical. I don't want to take advantage. I don't want to use another. I always look at myself. I always take responsibility – often to my detriment because I haven't been good at holding the other person accountable.

Unhook

How can you hold someone accountable who won't be accountable? You cannot. But I didn't want to be alone. I didn't want to be abandoned. If I pick up the slack, can there still be a connection? So, I have put up with too much. Why? Because I have been taught that to be in relationship, I have to compromise myself. I have not known anything else. This part of me I have had to outgrow. This understanding is not valid. It is not true. I will be okay no matter what. I won't put up with unacceptable behavior. Underneath, I would carry the load, but that comes from a good part of me, a connector, and too much fear. The fear is not true. I won't do it anymore.

Our Family

I am angry that you abandoned our cats. Hank and Sassy. Hank, whom we adopted when he was about six weeks old. Hank who was loyal and true. Hank who was mischievous and playful. Sassy, an abused cat who adopted us, a cat with big needs. After you left, you never saw them again.

When Hank got sick, shortly after you left, you had said you would stop in to see him. You never did. They have both since died. I held Sassy as she was injected to put her to sleep, to put her out of her pain.

Watched her little pink nose twitch, and then her tense body relax as she let go. I cried for her without you.

Hank was like our child. Maybe you didn't feel that way. Hank deserved so much more than being ignored by you, abandoned by you. What would have happened if we had human children together? Would you also have abandoned them too?

Casting off My Guilt

Under my anger, I feel so sad. I learned I didn't really know you. I wanted to stay friends. I was willing to do things differently. You weren't. This one is bad on you. This one you ruined. I'm sad at the choices you made. So sad at what you did to the love we once had.

I am mad at you and disappointed in you for how you behaved. I am mad at you for thinking I was bad. I am mad at you for mistreating me. I am mad at you for turning from someone I loved into someone I couldn't even like. You did not live up to your promise.

I've focused on understanding. I've focused on being kind. I've focused on forgiveness towards you. But what about me? My anger is leading me to compassion for myself.

Redraw

I never realized how damaged you were. I knew you were damaged, but how you treated me is not how the you I thought I knew would treat anybody. I have had to redraw my picture of you.

Like my dad, there was a good dad and a bad dad. I put up with the bad dad because I didn't have any choice and because I loved the good dad. And so it is with you, too – there is the good you and the bad you. It was confusing. Now it is clear. You decided to punish. That is how you used your creative power, how you influenced the world. That is the poison you spread.

I thought you were better than that. You weren't. You were smaller and more damaged than I realized. And I accepted way too little. You taught me to be patient, to live without the connection I craved. That my life outside of our relationship was where my energy needed to go, and ultimately, you taught me that I wasn't responsible for you or your feelings. You taught me that I wanted more. Your anger wasn't about me. It was about your own ego and your own dark feelings. Your meanness wasn't about me. It was about your own smallness. You tried to put your shame on me, make me feel as if I were greedy, as if I were bad. None of that was true. None of it was about money. It was about having value. It was about standing up for myself. Standing up to you nearly killed me. It wrecked my immune system, left me open to what would be next.

Self-Love

I had to spend a lot of years with not enough to get to a point where I was willing to leave to have more. I guess I had a lot to learn and a lot to transform in myself. I guess I was used to "making do or making it work." Sometimes, we just don't know better. Or even if we do, we cannot find the part of ourselves that can say no. I couldn't.

I am slowly stepping out of the tight clutches of fear. I see that I can create what I need in my life.

I couldn't do it right away because, deep down, I didn't really believe I deserved more. But now I do.

In the end, you taught me more about self-love than actually loving me. My love stopped being love for you. I had to love myself to get out. I had to love myself to get through how you treated me. I couldn't bow to your reality. It wasn't mine, and I didn't want it.

A Moment

I remember the moment I knew it was over. I had been waiting and waiting for you to have a break from work so we could reconnect. And finally, you did; you had a break. But you had no interest in reconnecting. We were at a party together, with your brother. I might as well have gone alone. I knew then I was finished with us. I knew that the years and years of couples counseling did not save us. I knew I wasn't waiting for you anymore.

My Truth

I had loved you – I really did. I was crazy about you for a while. And I cared about your life and that you found fulfillment. I supported you in the important areas. I always wanted the best for you. I encouraged you to develop your creativity. I told you not to take work you didn't want, that happiness was more important than driving yourself – you closed your ears and took that work anyway. You did as you wanted and chose to resent me instead of finding balance. Pushing instead of flowing. Closing instead of opening. You lost your way.

I still want you to be happy – even now, even after all of this. I know you think I am "bad," but I cannot do anything about that. I had to walk my own truth.

I get that it wasn't yours. I am sorry that I had to leave you to find all of my happiness. I am sorry I didn't do it the way you wanted me to. I am sorry that my rejection of you caused you so much pain. I am sorry that you could not still be friends or even friendly. I am sorry that my leaving you hurt you. I'm sorry for the earthquake I created in your psyche. I'm sorry for the shame I triggered. And yet, it is your shame and your responsibility.

Forgive me for hurting you. Forgive me for choosing to walk my own path and leaving you. Forgive me for not knowing how to work it out with you. Forgive me for giving up on you and on us. Forgive me for not wanting what you wanted. Forgive me for not appreciating the way you gave to me.

It must hurt when your best is not good enough. I get that. And your best wasn't good enough. Maybe it wasn't your best. Not that I didn't appreciate the ways that you supported and helped me. I did. Materially was how you gave. It was a valuable gift for me. You supported me as I built new parts of myself, new skills, and now, from that, I live in a new world. You helped me become somebody who can give to others even more. But I wanted more. I wanted more of you. And that wasn't available for me.

Thank you for all the learning I gained by knowing you. Thank you for helping me start a new career. Thank you for caring, even if you often could not show it. Thank you for being a part of my life for a long time. Thank you for the moments that you were my friend.

Gift

I cannot hear. Cannot see.

Caught.

Trapped.

Your soft pink energy. You wrap around me.

Sweetness.

You enter my body. My cells.

Your knowing. You whisper to me.

It will be okay. It will be okay.

Open your eyes. Know what must be.

Begin to put yourself back together.

I can hear you.

My spirit child.

A gift. A love.

Spirit Child

I knew the moment it happened. I started screaming. Then sobbing. I knew.

"I won't cum inside of you," he had said. He did. How could he do that? How did I let him?

The weight of that time heavy. I was not yet someone who could say no. I was not yet someone who had pushed the heavy blanket of my weaknesses aside, weaknesses that developed during my childhood and adolescence. A mix of nature and nurture. Of karma and the flow of lives working themselves out.

It was a wake-up call. Bigger than the previous ones.

My body felt different immediately. I missed my next period. I don't remember the pregnancy test, but I do remember Planned Parenthood. The young girls in trouble sitting in the waiting room. My boyfriend offered to marry me. I looked at him as if he were crazy. A crack addict to help raise a baby I didn't want and wouldn't be able to take care of. A man emaciated with a pot belly and bad teeth from his drug use. A man who did not honor his word. No. I would not marry him.

Communion

"I can't keep you," I said to this spirit hovering around me. She had not yet descended into my body.

"You are not supposed to keep me," she replied. "I came to wake you up, to make you look at your life and your weaknesses, your choices. I have other places to be. But I love you, so I came to help you."

Your cells began to magically multiply in me. My breasts enlarged. I developed food cravings. But we both knew you would leave soon.

Earn Your Keep

In the kitchen at my parents' house one afternoon, my father announced out of the blue that if my sister or I ever got pregnant, he and my mother would raise the baby. I was probably in my early twenties and was visiting home. My father who was against abortion. My father who both controlled and resented us. His resentment a heavy weight on our lives. A glass of milk accidentally spilled at the dinner table by one of us. My father's face red with rage. He yells. We are bad, careless, wasteful. He sacrificed for that glass of milk. The metaphor of our lives. Stupid kid.

Everyone had to earn their own keep. The chickens laid eggs, but the young roosters only ate. My father put a sock over their heads, held their struggling bodies to the log chopping block, and brought the axe down. Held the jerking body still. He did this despite the nightmares that visited him afterward.

I remember sitting at the dinner table. We were eating a rooster we knew – a friend with a name. My siblings and I were sobbing.

My father would start talking about all the roosters; there were too many, his resentment of all the mouths to feed. He would announce that the next day, he was going to kill them. My siblings and I, at one time, knowing what was to happen the following day, hid the young roosters in the coal shed. We saved some of them for a while.

I was not present during the murders of these beings with names. I could not be a part of the murder of my companions. I did not see the world as he did, that everyone had to earn their own keep. Even then, I believed we could be here because of grace, because each being had beauty, because there was space for us.

This the man who assumed he and my mother would raise the baby should my sister or I get pregnant. The presumption that it was his choice.

More Than a Footprint
"No," I said inside. "Never." After my childhood with them. A childhood that included rage and violence. Hitting and punitive actions. That my father, who felt we stopped him from his blossoming, should have anything to do with a being I brought into the world.

Was I that voiceless? Yes. You raised me to be voiceless. You raised me to acquiesce. You raised me to be the footprint shaped to your foot. I would never willingly allow you to do that to another. Growing up with you, I had no power, but I had eyes. I saw the wounding you caused. No, you do not get to make that choice. You do not get to dictate here.

Throughout my father's proclamation about raising the child if my sister or I ever were pregnant, my mother was silent. I do not know what she thought.

I did not tell them. I didn't even consider it.

Thank You, Spirit Child

My boss dropped me off and picked me up from Planned Parenthood. I could not trust that my boyfriend would be sober and available to show up. And I could not go alone. I was grateful to her. I still am.

The procedure... a sucking sensation. The sucking out of a potential embodied being. She would stay in the ethers. I, staring at the ceiling, counting the ceiling tiles. Empty feeling. Later, the intense cramping and the bleeding.

I had known years before that I would never want to bring a child into this world. I remember as a teenager walking down the dirt road after one of my parents had gotten mad, the manta, *never get married, never have kids, never get married, never have kids*, circling around in my head.

I talked to the spirit of the child. I asked her if it was okay for her to not come in at this time and not with me. I knew what her purpose was. I knew she had come as an angel to wake me up. I knew her spirit never expected to be born. I was at peace with this.

Because of this knowing, there was never any sense of guilt.

You were my one and only abortion. You whom I love. You, whom I have deep gratitude for. You who I will never know in the flesh this lifetime. I never again needed a wakeup call that big. Thank you, Spirit Child, for your gift to me.

✴

Home

A warm hand holding

the comfort of two bodies touching

a nourishment eternal

that reaches across

each moment.

I did not know

how the space of years

the warp of time

would gift me

a love

called home.

✻

Husband Home

After all the losses, the disappointments, the shedding of what was, the removing of what did not work, there was room for something new to be born. This union with Mike, my second husband, is different than all that was before. I was luckier this time. If you could call it that. Not luck, but something else. The release of what is not true. The tiny space of authenticity, nurtured and allowed to grow. From that, I found someone who also is my home, my protection and safety, my comfort. Perhaps if I were a saint or more fully enlightened, home would be a self-sufficient and internal place in this ever-shifting and often trauma-filled world. I know that we are all here on a very temporary basis, and clutching at the temporal isn't the best strategy for security. But I am human and cannot imagine life without my husband.

I notice how the skin on his hands is thin and almost translucent, soft to the touch. They are delicate and have their own kind of beauty. Not the robust beauty of youth but the soft beauty of age that comes from a life well lived with grace and generosity. I hope to spend many more years with him, chattering into the night, working together, and being the team that we are.

And so I hold onto my husband as I also seek god and a way to survive our transient world. I seek to know that there is goodness beyond the home I have with my husband. Someday, death will pry my hungry fingers away. I will look up towards eternity and the multitude of stars scattered across an ebony field and wonder how to fill the space he created; the home I feel with him.

Perhaps I can prepare? Perhaps I can trust that even as I adore and find gratitude for our time together, this little speck of home we have carved out together is more enduring than it appears, that it will be a rock for me even after it has evaporated, that our time together is as big as the eons of the universe. That I will feel his presence after he passes. That I will grow into a bigger being. That our relationship will be inside me as an experience that cannot be taken away and a knowing that becomes integral to who I am.

Newly Freed

Releasing our binds is not for the faint-hearted. Our courage in doing so allows us to cast off the mold we were formed in, to reform in a new and truer shape. Like Inanna, we return to the surface, newly empowered. Our being newly freed. Our presence stronger. Our inner fire strengthened. Our equanimity increases, and the divine flows through and radiates. There is magic here in this process. An alchemy that occurs as our souls interact with life, as our courage helps us sort and release, as we step more fully into our powerful selves and new life steps forward to meet us. As I grow and heal, so do you, for each of our journeys opens the way for others to step forward onto their path. And in that, there is wonder.

✵

6
The Call to Heal Others

Witches do not need to fix problems. Witches fix the energy AROUND problems. Then the problems fix themselves.
~ Dacha Avelin

✴

Compassion

After the dark night of the soul, after I began to develop skills, there was another call, the call to help others heal. My compassion, which got me entangled with unhealed others, was also part of my calling. The call to use what I was learning, the rebuilding of the self, the knowing that we have the power to create ourselves and help others do the same.

I was called to heal. I was called to help others heal. By giving what I most needed, I answered this call. What else was there for me to do but offer myself to those who needed me? Healing others is giving back. To see beauty where others do not. To help organize chaos into meaning.

It is taking pieces of our hearts and giving, loaning them to others. The heart regenerates. There is no loss. Only more hearts beating firmly. Reverberating. Encompassing. Loving.

For me, it also means recognizing that I am here and that I am who I am because of the help I have received. This is such an important statement to say to myself.

I am who I am because of the help I have received.

I didn't just heal. I used books written by people. I had contact with people and animals who provided love and support. I saw skilled and caring therapists. I took workshops and studied. I was guided and led.

When choosing a graduate school, I looked at a list of schools. My eyes went to a name on the list. Pacifica Graduate Institute. I had never heard of that school and knew nothing about it. I felt a knowing that was where I would go. It was the only graduate school I applied to. I was accepted. I entered the Jungian world of dreams, depth psychology, and myth. I began to formally learn about healing.

❋

Therapist Witch

I put my toe tentative out.
What am I? Who?

Behind me
a wall of learning.
Solid, tall, dense.

And history
like the striations of rock fused.
Freud and Jung
Winnicott and Rogers
Kohut and Ogden.

Other skills, more ancient
began to speak, to say,
let me out
let me be
let me live.

let me see,
let me tell
let me heal.

Drawn together
magnetized
these pieces flew
coalesced.

> Old magic and new magic
> melt into each other, fuse
>
> Like an enchantment
> like a squall
> like the pink cloud floating over a blue water
> I began to see
> myself.

※

The Threat of Internal Power

I also entered the realm of witches. Witches are healers and people of power. They are agentic, meaning they have the power to control or create their own goals, actions, and destinies. They have the power to remake the self, becoming a co-creator with the divine forces. They are visionaries and oftentimes portals to the spiritual. And they operate according to spiritual, not human standards. Because of the internal power of an integrated witch, we are threats to conventional thought that believed (and may continue to believe) women should raise children, manage a household, and be subservient to their husbands. Magic was sometimes merged with the idea of the devil's work.

Historically, those caught in conventional and religious thought were threatened by what they did not understand and could not control. Humans are often fear-based beings.

Those who did not fit into preconceived boxes could be scapegoated. Witches, being outside of conventional understanding, were the calamity. The suffering engendered was astronomical, destructive, and criminal.

The talent and knowledge destroyed unfathomable. Even today, witches are not only often scoffed at and ridiculed but, in some areas, still murdered.

But from that dispirited history, we re-emerge in the present day. We step up yet again to raise our voices. To say, I am here. To offer our gifts to others. Our insight, our ability to shift outcomes, to infuse situations, people, environments with love. My therapeutic work with others was my way of offering this gift, of offering what I had learned on my journey, both in this life and before.

Heart Broke Open

Although I worked with many populations, individuals, families, and adults, my work with children most deeply affected me. The children broke my heart open yet again, for our world, for these little beings with painful challenges that lay ahead years before they would have autonomy and find themselves. I saw how long the journey would be for them.

Liminal Space

My with these children occured in liminal space, the threshold between two realities, where change occurs, often the boundary between our world and another. Liminal space could also be called "between worlds."

Witches do much of their work in the threshold between worlds. Between the world that is or was and the world being created. Standing between what is or was and what will be, can be scary. It can also be exhilarating. There is great power here. The work done in these spaces literally opens doorways to new ways of being.

This is not the place of cognitive behavioral therapy but of the open space where the imagination can dance. Play occurs here, for in play, we are in an imaginary reality. Much healing work is done in this threshold space.

When I did some EMDR (Eye Movement Desensitization and Reprocessing) sessions with Steven, a talented therapist, we worked together in a liminal space. As I recounted trauma that I had experienced, and he moved an object back and forth for my eyes to follow (to help facilitate brain integration), he helped me follow each new image. We would start with what happened. I would say it out loud. Then he would ask what was happening next. As I followed these images, they morphed and changed. We departed from history and internally, new events occurred. Instead of being afraid of my raging father, I found myself standing up to him, becoming more powerful than him. These images grew in my psyche. They nourished me and allowed me to change my relationship to the events that had caused me trauma.

✵

Transitional World

When I worked with children, our work was not in their regular reality of questions and answers, of the left-brain logic that gives order to our everyday lives. The work we did was not rational and orderly. Logic did not apply. Instead, we stepped into a different space, what Winnicott – the groundbreaking twentieth-century pediatrician and psychoanalyst – would call the space of Transitional Objects and Transitional Phenomena. This is a magical world where a child imaginatively uses an object to play with, attach to, and reduce stress in processes that, over time, form a bridge to relate to others in a new way.

An object, like a blanket, can become an emotional link to a family member and allow the child to tolerate a temporary absence.

In this space, two people can play without being in the understandable world, without trying to make sense of things. Instead, mystery, ambiguities, and fantasy can be experienced. Feelings can be acted out. An internal world can be made manifest, so it is experienced and, in doing so, becomes enacted and spoken.

Similarly, many cultures have healing ceremonies and rituals in this space. Navajo Sand painting is one example of this process, as well as the Drypainting of Tibetan and Buddhist monks. The paintings are not made as objects of art but are instead a process, part of a healing ritual. The Medicine Man chants, asking the Holy People to come into the painting while letting the colored sands flow from his fingers in one of the many traditional designs.

These paintings are not static objects but living and spiritual beings to be treated with reverence. As the healing chant continues, the patient will be asked to sit on the painting. Later, the painting is destroyed as it has absorbed the illness.

The act of creating the medicine art provides a portal so that spirits have a place to enter and heal. These enactments are not permanent... not intended to hang on the wall of a house or a museum. They are temporary, a ritual that moves energy and facilitates transformation. They create a space or threshold where healing can occur.

✵

ENOUGH

There is enough
if we share
if I take my arms
fold them around you.

There is enough
if we believe
the yellow brick road
unwinds, spirals and
Glenda from above
her pink dress luminous
whispers her good words.

There is enough
if we frolic, dance,
beads of sweat
and sparks of fire
the bodies sway
celebration
of spirit.

There is enough
when we see
who we are.

Cloaked

It is the early and mid-2000s. I am working with children. A dark cloud of depression descended and enveloped me, plunging me back into the feelings of powerlessness of my own childhood. These vulnerable beings were caught in situations or family structures hurting them. Parents at war, unseeing, or cold with hearts that could not be reached. Narcissism, Hatred. Addictions, Violence, Wounds.

Working with these children was simple. Working with them was torturous. It was simple because they needed acceptance and love more than anything else. That was easy to give. They just needed to be affirmed, to have someone pay attention to their feelings, their inner lives.

It was torturous because they were innocent. Because I fell in love with them, saw the limits of what I could do. Because an hour a week might give them nourishment, but it could not change their lives, the conditions they lived in. A heaviness settled, cloaked me. I could not lift it. It did not leave until I stopped working with these children. They put me face to face with my struggle, with my limitations. My struggle with the path of pain many walk through. My struggle with my history.

Enactments

One child. Five or six years old. Acting out, disobedient. His mother adored him. His father, mostly absent, was inconsistent and violent when he was present. This child had witnessed severe domestic violence. He had watched his father harm his mother. Powerless.

He could not save her. He could not stop his father. He could not deal with what he had experienced, what it triggered, how it made him feel.

We played together. We took all the cushions, the furniture, stuffed animals, other toys and made forts, waged battles, and wars in my office. We enacted scenarios. We killed and took prisoners. We saved and rescued. We hid and were found. It was very active. It was hard work. I kept up with him, stayed with his energy, his enactments. Made statements to help him integrate the voices of his imagination with his reality.

He loved this time playing with me. We did not talk much. It was all acted out. His feelings were made apparent with each scenario and attack. It was a challenging therapy for me. I am a talker, a discusser, an uncoverer of hidden patterns. Instead, I had to be willing to deconstruct my office and allow him to lead. Because this is what worked for him.

Sometimes, I would talk to him for a while or read him a story. However, the enactments of situations and physical expression dominated each session.

This child enacted protecting his mother. He enacted a power he did not have in real life. He needed to know that he could "kill" what was bad and save what was vulnerable. He needed to do this because he did not know how to metabolize what he had lived through, the fear he had felt, the powerlessness and shame. His anger. He needed to express his confusion and jumble of feelings. He needed to be more than a bystander of his parents' relationship, his mother's desperation, his father's addictions, and violence.

A Bind

We often love those people who harm us. His father. This boy was in that bind. He wanted to be loved, but he could not be obedient. He had seen too much that was intolerable to him. He did not know what to do with the message about power. He did not know what to do with his pain, his anger.

I did not ask that he talk about his feelings. I did not tell him to be different or tell him how to deal with his feelings. He was too young and not that kind of a child.

I had to trust that this play was helping him. I had to trust that the imagination is one way of healing, that not everybody is verbal or willing to discuss what is troubling them or even consciously aware of what is bothering them. I had to trust that what we were doing together was meaningful. I had to let go of the illusion of control and be willing to see what emerged.

His mother reported him improving. He was happier and more willing to listen to her after each session. As she was doing her work in her own life, he was also doing his.

✺

Abundance

We cut the pie,

ate, stuffed our cheeks full,

juice running down

our faces.

A burst of delight, flavor.

Apple slices baked golden soft.

Raisin, rum, and cinnamon.

Crust butter flaky.

Mouth-melting goodness.

We have enough.

We are enough.

Love Pie

Each child demanded a different type of interaction, often a mix of listening, talking, and play.

Sometimes, I wrote them a story about a character who was just like them or read them a story from a book of therapeutic stories (*Therapeutic Stories that Teach and Heal* by Nancy Davis). When I wrote them a story about a character facing the same dilemma they were struggling with, they often were captivated. They wanted to hear that story over and over. It helped them make sense of their lives.

In the book of therapeutic stories, my favorite and most read story was about a pie. Every time a slice was taken and given to someone, the pie would grow that slice back. The pie was never going to be eaten up. It was never going to disappear. It would always be available. I explained to the child that the pie was just like love. There would always be more. An early and needed introduction to the abundance of love.

Feeling as if there is not enough is common. These children were often not loved in a way that was nourishing. They needed to know that there was enough, that they were enough, that the pie could regenerate and would not get used up. That the love they did not get was available somehow. That there was enough love for everyone. That we generate love. It is not a limited commodity.

Hero's Journey

I think of the parents caught in the flatland of outer reality, with no interest or understanding of why their children were misbehaving or that they were suffering. They wanted me to take their child and make them behave. Make them listen. Tell them what to do. Put them in the good kid box.

They had no knowledge of the mythology of being human. Of the hero's journey and how we must navigate through external and internal obstacles to full functioning. Of how each of us is so often confronted with situations that are not only difficult but seemingly impossible.

The way through never comes from outer control. It comes from helping that being navigate the internal struggle, helping them make sense of their feelings and begin to find a greater sense of wholeness.

✵

NOURISHMENT

She who sees
through her soul's tender flame.
Who creates shelter, protection
from the storm, the harsh chilling wind.

She who nourishes the unnourished
with a warm, tender touch.
Who creates a moment
of safety.

She who implants a memory
and keeps the flame of spirit burning.
Who knows what is needed.

Touchstone

I am very young. First grade. My hand is folding into the soft and perfumed hand of a woman with skin the color of café latte. I love how she smells. Her warm presence.

It is recess. Kids are yelling, screaming, shrieking, running. They are rough. There are shards of glass on the dirt and paved areas of the playground. There is nowhere for me to be.

She holds my hand, and I feel safe.

I don't remember playing at recess. I remember her soft presence. I remember the warmth of her hand.

I was a shy and lonely child. I was afraid of people, fearful of life, and too sensitive for this world for these loud children.

I carried my memory of this woman whose name I do not remember inside me through the years. Her soft hand holding mine, her kind countenance, this woman who stayed out on the playground during recess. A moment of comfort in a world that seemed harsh to me. She saw me. She saw how I needed to be loved. While the other children were in the midst of havoc, she gave me love by being with me.

The memory of her holding my hand has emerged periodically and helped me know there was kindness available.

The hand that holds is the hand that makes it okay. It is the hand that lets us know we are not alone. The hand that holds is connected to the heart.

What she gave to me, I have given to others.

Shared Tears

While I was a Marriage and Family Therapist Intern, several places I worked were at schools where I saw children and teenagers for therapy. At one school, the teachers decided who needed to spend an hour a week with me for that semester. They usually picked the kids who were acting out. But in one case, a teacher picked a lost child. It was in the days when we still used the word "retarded."

I can still clearly see her being-ness, her face, her quiet sadness.

Even now, after many years. She was maybe eight, nine, or ten years old. Short and rotund. Dark-skinned round face. Big brown sad eyes. They thought she was "slow." She didn't fit into her grade. Her teacher saw how withdrawn she was, that she did not talk, and knew she needed support, so I spent an hour a week with her for a while.

I met her mother once. Laughing, jolly, vibrant – but not at all tuned into her introverted, sensitive daughter.

A lost child. She did not speak to me for a long time. We played games. I would sit with her, see her, be kind to her. I didn't pressure her to be different. I didn't ask anything of her. I simply was with her.

One day, this child started talking to me. She told me a story. Her family had a new dog. This dog attacked their cat. The cat was her friend. The first time he went for the cat, he injured the cat. The cat got away. The next day, the dog caught and killed the cat. We stared into each other's eyes as she told me this story. Her round eyes filled with big, wet tears. Mine filled also.

I could not fix it. I could not do anything but sit with this child, heart to heart, eyes to eyes. I shared her grief. I felt her pain. My heart broke with hers.

She had found love where she could and then lost it. Her cat friend killed. Unseen, nobody had intervened to help her. Nobody saw her loss. Nobody cared enough to help the cat, to help her.

I knew this girl. I knew this story. It wasn't my story, but it was close enough. The story of the forgotten child, the one who wasn't seen.

These children. I spent an hour a week with them. Gave them all of me while I was with them. Then they went back to their homes. Their homes that would not change. I went back to mine, depressed. I could not save them. I could only give them a touchstone. A moment or two, they might carry inside. A seed that might someday receive what it needed and open in a new environment, a new moment.

※

The In-Between Space

I know this place. Sacred threshold.
Where my work unfolds.
Open, the tingly breeze of insight blows through.

The walls are made of love. The air of grace.
The spirits speak, their voices a light flutter,
a flash of insight, a whisper, a tension in the gut.

Release together.
We let go of what has held us,
even as it has bound us.
Free fall, it is not scary.

Love and grace,
ancestors and spirits
shimmer around us.

We hear new voices.
See new vistas.
Patterns emerge.

Oh, look. Yes, and that. See.

Maybe I can be more. Maybe I can be free.
Unhooked from what has caught.
Unraveled from fear
into pure sight.
Into a new world.

Untangling Love

I was working with a young teenager whose family was part of a violent gang. As we walked down the hallway to my office, he stopped in front of a poster of trees and stared at it. He said that he liked how it made him feel. He said he wished he could be there, in those trees, in that sense of peace.

As a child, he had seen one of his relatives murder a member of another gang. Another family member was in prison. He was in a school for "emotionally disturbed teenagers." That was what he knew.

This child, despite his environment and the trauma he had hardened to, resonated with the beauty and sense of peace of those trees. We recognize what we innately have the potential to be: love, beauty, peace. In a sense, we are tuning devices. Our tuning capabilities may be in chaos, a tangled knot, or we may be able to intuit, feel, and even radiate ideas or qualities such as peace or wisdom.

Walls

The kids I saw at this school were sad kids, angry kids, kids with messed up homes. Kids who were acting out for various reasons. But underneath all their acting out, they were kids who felt hurt and rejected. They felt like failures. Some of them had erected enormous walls around themselves. These were not obedient children. They were not the kids who got A's. They could not be forced to be what adults demanded of them. They didn't care about other people's rules. Other people and their rules had failed them.

They were doing their best and they were sometimes difficult to reach.

The supervisor in charge of the therapists was very strict. I didn't like him. I didn't like his philosophy, his judgment, or how he looked down on the kids. I didn't like his authoritarianism. I didn't like his rigidity. He felt the kids needed boundaries. Perhaps they did. But I felt they needed more: someone open, non-judgmental, and willing to listen. These two things were often in conflict.

Trusted

I often took the older kids individually with me on a walk, and we would talk about their lives. I took them out to get them moving and free up their energy, to get them feeling less trapped than sitting in a rectangular room faced with a person who wanted them to obey, to talk – to "do" therapy, to expose themselves. I took them out so we could notice the weather, feel the sun, see the trees, hear them rustle in the breeze, the hills rising into the hazy air in the distance.

In a sense, I became a trusted adult friend. This was something they didn't have. I was somebody they would sometimes share their hopes and dreams with. I was somebody who would listen. I provided a place where, hopefully, these kids would talk about their dilemmas, their concerns. Or sometimes just playing games with the younger ones without judgment or pressure was what they needed. This was, at times, the therapy.

A Smoke

A few of them would sometimes smoke a cigarette. This was against the rules. I had a choice. I could enforce the rules and, in their minds, be one of the people who focused on what they should and should not do, those who made the rules more important than their feelings. Or not.

I wasn't silent. I brought up that cigarettes were not healthy for them. I brought up that we could get in trouble. It wasn't a difficult choice. "Meet the client where they are at" is one of the golden standards of therapy. I decided the one additional cigarette they smoked that week with me was not worth the cost of not being able to connect with them. My job and interest were healing their spirits rather than being the enforcer of their obedience. That knowing was my director, not the man stifled by limitations who hired me.

Other Realities

I gave those children what I needed when I was their age. I survived my childhood and teenage years because I found love with the animals that surrounded me. They accepted me. They had time for me. I felt safe with them. They expressed love towards me, and I towards them. I also survived because I read. Reading let me know there were realities other than the one I felt trapped in. I read voraciously. I read to escape my life and be in another place. I read to find comfort. I read to find a place in which I could reside. I read to know that more existed than the life I was in. I needed to know there was more kindness in the world than what I experienced.

When these children were with me, they were in a different reality than their usual world. Who I was with these children let them know they could have a different kind of relationship than the ones they knew. Their relationship with me was different than their relationship with their teachers, parents, and peers. It had space in it. I didn't have to be the one who disciplined them. But I could talk about their choices and potential consequences. And while our therapy might not "fix" their presenting issue, it allowed them some room to breathe, to consider, to be.

Open Space

As some of these children developed trust in me, we could begin to talk about what was difficult for them. We could begin exhuming some of what they were struggling with, bringing it up into the air, the light, so it would stop festering. Not every kid went there; developing trust with some of them would take far longer than the time I had. But some of them did step into the open space I provided.

In a sense, this work was similar to making friends with a wild animal. Each unique and beautiful, but cautious, guarded. Relational trust develops over time with consistent care. With the offer of gifts, food, caring, and kindness. With the hope that these ingredients and this relationship will allow the bud to open into a fuller bloom.

Only when we feel safe and cared for can we journey into the darker parts of ourselves to unearth, tend, and ultimately make whole and transform those parts into something more whole and less fractured.

Our journey into the light is equally a journey down into the depths. If you position yourself as a being of love, meaning a part of the divine spark of life, then the journey to wholeness will ask that you also explore the components of yourself that are not about love. Pushing away the dark parts of yourself will not bring you to wholeness.

Caught

These children were caught. They didn't know how to navigate through their lives in a way that was smooth or abundant. They were already wounded. They were already struggling. Something they needed wasn't yet accessible. Whether it was love, support, or something else. They were not yet adults. They were being forced to do "therapy." They were told they were dysfunctional, bad, not right. They pushed against these messages. This was their method of survival. They were not old enough to begin to untangle what was caught.

My Choice

When we are caught, we don't know which way to go, what to choose, or even how to choose. This is when "untangling" becomes the most productive choice.

Untangling is the path of rebuilding one's structure, making one's clarity of being more important than any outer achievement. It is not the easy path to obvious and visible success, for that path does not exist for one who is tangled. The path of untangling requires the ability to see and honor oneself, for the work being done will not be applauded by others – they often do not see it. But you will have a richer life for doing it.

Untangling that which is snared, stuck, and twisted is a growth choice. This has been my choice, my destiny, and my path, and doing so has become a massive force in my life.

The choice to dig deep, to untangle what was stopping me, reducing clarity, or causing pain, made over and over again, is what has allowed me to be the self I now am.

Untangling is a journey. This journey starts inside yourself. It starts with learning how to honor yourself and others. It includes trusting that you can work with what you have been given, where you are at, and make it meaningful and purposeful. It is the interior quest of going into the psyche and tending to the various parts of ourselves. The hurt parts, the protector parts, the wily parts, the parts that wish the self-harm. As we untangle, we become clearer. We become able to be a more solid presence. We become freer and can more easily express ourselves and flow with our lives.

We have power in the present moment. In each moment, there is always a choice. Even if no choice is available in the external world, there is an internal choice. How do I choose to view this? What attitude do I choose to take?

Often, our choices are between what is life-affirming and what is not. Sometimes, we choose the less life-affirming path. That is significant because we experience what does not work, what does not fill us with joy. Yet, in the next moment, we may again have another choice. At any point, our choices may change. What and how we choose becomes our path.

Linking

Our feelings are entryways that allow us to better understand ourselves. As we open into difficult feelings, we begin remembering ourselves. It is as if we live out of one part of ourselves and have put the others, the parts that hold complicated and unwanted feelings, away. These aspects sometimes jump out unbidden, but we do not know them. We live out of a fragment of ourselves instead of a cohesive whole. We are a segregated being. And as the microcosm, so is the macrocosm. We contribute to a world where certain things are not accepted or are pushed away, whether it is a feeling or somebody else's rights. We try to put what we don't want in a tidy container. Like those children. We try to control from the outside instead of letting the internal life lead.

I have an advantage here. I am naturally a digger and a burrower. I instinctively root out and explore the troubled parts of myself. I cannot imagine doing otherwise. I wasn't always this way. Luckily, life created some relational disasters for me and caused me to begin to look at myself, to start the task of sorting through the aspects of myself that simply did not work for all of me.

Psyche's Support

Understanding the task of sorting through our profound and often overwhelming issues can be helped by looking at the myth of Psyche and Eros and specifically at Psyche's interactions with Aphrodite. Psyche was a beautiful woman. The Goddess Aphrodite was jealous of Psyche and gave her many impossible tasks.

The first was for Psyche to sort through a vast granary filled with many kinds of seeds. Psyche was instructed to sort through them by sundown. Psyche was beside herself, crying and completely overwhelmed. As she cried, an army of ants arrived, and they began to sort the seeds. By nightfall, the task was complete. Psyche was not able to sort the seeds herself.

She needed assistance, and in her case, because she had a clear intention with integrity, help arrived.

I think of a couple I had worked with. As the male partner began to allow himself more vulnerability (which was necessary), the female partner began to feel disgust. Although she wanted him more attuned to her, to feelings, to connection, she could not tolerate the very ingredient that would get him there. Her work would be to look at her fear of a "soft" man. She would need to unpack many experiences she had around her father and her ideas of being protected by the masculine element and let down by gentleness, which she saw as weakness. Deep issues will not heal on their own. Yet, beginning the journey of looking more deeply at ourselves and untangling ourselves can be overwhelming and confusing. We often don't know where to start.

Reborn

I am sitting in my office. In front of me, out the window, the grass unfolds, the water ripples, the sky enfolds, the sun's light spreads. I close my eyes. I can see the light through my closed eyelids. I can feel the lightness of the air. I notice my breathing, my lungs filling, my chest expanding, lifting, and releasing. How my body fits into the chair. The areas of pressure. I take a moment and just be. Allow myself to experience what is in this moment.

And then I set an intention. I breathe in the fullness of the air, and as I breathe out, I say to myself, "*May I find balance today. May I be in peace. May I release what is not mine. May I assist where it is appropriate. Thank you, god and goddess.*" I feel peaceful as I say this. I trust this intention will help inform my day, propel and shift energy so that it is realized.

When we set the intention to love ourselves, to love others, and to look deeply into the areas that are tangled, we often find a way to do so. Our intentions are powerful. We become more integrated and step more fully into the process of reclaiming our whole selves; we begin to be lighter. We begin to be more whole. What has died within us comes to life and has an opportunity to re-engage consciously. A dialogue ensues. We become happier. We begin to love all of ourselves. The quality of our connections becomes filled with more love. Our life and life itself become fuller.

※

Unfurled

The armadillo has a thick skin.
She rolls up in a ball
when threatened.

It is not easy,
to eat, drink water
play
like this.

Imagine yourself
unrolled all the way
like a soft carpet of grass or
an open flower spreading
soft petals and scent.
A small heaven
unfurled.

Creating Safety

Years ago, in graduate school, our class did an exercise of visualizing a safe place. We sat in folding chairs placed in a semi-circle. Our instructor guided us in a breathing exercise to ground us. She helped us notice our bodies, notice the space around us, and finally, asked us to bring into our minds a safe place.

As students becoming therapists, we needed access to our own safe place to work with others. Those we would be working with would need a solid and stable presence to help them through their confusions, traumas, and challenges.

Not everyone could find a safe place. For some, a sense of safety simply did not exist. Others found their safety alone, often in nature. Still others could find it in relation to someone specific, for example, a pet or grandparent. My safe space was in my bed. It was where I could be alone with my thoughts.

Yet, even though that came up for me as a safe space, I remember being afraid to sleep unless my back was to the wall. I needed to be facing the room and door. I needed to know I could see whatever or whoever might be coming. I remember my father barging into my sister's and my room with his belt because we were talking at night. I don't remember him hitting us, although I know he sometimes did.

Why do we struggle so with safety? What makes us feel so unsafe?

All we have to do is look at our outer world, and it is clear why safety can be an issue. We have all experienced pain. And we are bombarded with images and stories of suffering and acts of cruelty.

Cruelty Free

I had been haunted by images before. Sometimes, it is a positive image. More often, though, it is an image that is horrible in some way. The image I am thinking of is of a little monkey being used for experiments. His hand is reaching out of his tiny cage. I can feel him reaching for love, for connection, reaching out of his cruel and unkind existence. The image haunts me because I can feel his pain, his need, his sadness, and his aloneness. It haunts me because this is not the world I wish to be a part of. The term "cruelty-free" was created for a reason. And yet we are surrounded by countless acts of cruelty to both animals and people, to forests, to the earth.

I grew up in a world where my feelings did not matter. My mother was somewhat disconnected from feelings. Feelings were complicated for her. My father was hypersensitive to his own feelings but often in a state where he was unconcerned with or unaware of the feelings of others. Animals other than pets were practically considered inanimate objects by the local people. Our neighbor drowned or asphyxiated the new batches of kittens each year and shot their family dog, Rocky, when he didn't want him anymore. Classmates told stories of hurting animals, and I heard and read other stories of horror not worth repeating.

Divide

Somehow, we don't think we are the same as others. It is as if we are real, and they are not. We have feelings and needs, and they do not. This divide of self and other spreads outward. The world becomes ego-centric and mostly about us. We become the center of the universe – and lose a sense of the interconnectedness of all of us.

Disconnected from ourselves, we cannot feel or know who we are. Disconnected from others, we cannot feel their needs, their discomfort.

I remember when I, my siblings, and our next-door neighbor and friends would camp outside in the cow pasture as teenagers – a chance to get away from our parents for a night. I listened to the large and lumbering bodies of the cows as they approached grazing. They had big, liquid brown eyes and mostly peaceful spirits. I enjoyed feeling their presence. I felt a communion with them that was soothing.

Yet we cut ourselves off from our connection with others as individuals, as a species, and as a society. I imagine it starts with hunting and eating others to survive. You either disconnect from the life you are going to kill, or you have a belief that it is okay.

Thank You

For me, what works is thanking the being who was sacrificed. Recognizing and honoring that life. It does not work for me to say, "They are just animals." It does not work for me to push part of myself away and not recognize or honor another being. It is not okay to leave a being reaching out of a cage with no one present to let that being know that it is not alone.

Disconnect

We all do it. Disconnect. Maybe not all the time, perhaps not usually. Maybe we started early. Sometimes, it is just a tiny part of ourselves that we have gotten rid of. Maybe someone hurt our feelings, and we "got rid of them" instead of staying with those feelings. Perhaps it was easier to get rid of our feelings than to know that our mother or father wasn't treating us with respect or love. Feelings can be painful. It can seem easier to avoid the pain of experiencing our feelings fully.

When we push away our emotions, the internal divide gets deeper. We stop knowing who we are. In a sense, we become "top-heavy" with excessive thought but not much feeling experience.

When we cannot feel, we cannot connect. We cannot care. Perhaps we can't take in the feelings of others, whether it is the cow out in the pasture or our partner or friend who is upset. Sometimes, our own upset feelings are the only ones that matter.

They take over, and we cannot see another's perspective.

Compassion

Compassion can only come through connection. Compassion for ourselves usually allows us to extend it outward to others. We connect with ourselves, with our own feelings and then extend that outward. If I can deeply experience myself, then perhaps I can spread that self-knowing and self-empathy to all others. It means no longer putting ourselves first. It means I want all children to go to better schools and have a meaningful and prosperous life, not just my children. It means not wanting anybody to suffer or starve or be beaten or be stopped by a "glass ceiling." It means we recognize that we are all in this together. Getting on top isn't the path to safety. Safety is only possible if we are all safe.

The Little Monkey

Love cannot be outmanoeuvred. We can open to it, or we can push it away. Love is not the cold, hard, and detached stare of someone who doesn't care. Love embraces. Isn't that the realm of the heart to be nurtured and cared about and related to? Isn't that what we all want?

We are all perpetrators in some way or another. We may hope the world will change, but it cannot without recognizing that the little monkey in the cage is also a part of each of us.

To create safety in a relationship, we have to be emotionally trustworthy. We have to learn to be there for each other. We have to reach our hand out to hold the hand of the other who is suffering.

The Beads

A necklace,
the gemstones brilliant
blues, ambers, and greens
corals and stone.

The fresh breeze
of color and light
texture and sound,
emanating uniqueness.

Strung together
each between the others
touching
enlivening
linking
part of a whole
yet individual.

Influencing,
offering
emitting
our beauty and light.

Beads

Like the beads in this book, the little gems of light strewn about, used to open and introduce us to a new thought or new story; we are also each a bead. A bit of light strung between others. Linked together, a necklace, special and unique. Will our bead shine, hold, nourish, tell a truth, or will it lie dull, cloaked, unable to transmit light and love to others? You can shine like a gem, shine through your heart, touch, enliven, love what is around you. You have this capacity. You are a vehicle for light. Use yourself well.

More Human = Compassion

Our witch qualities make us more human. We are sensitized not only to what we need but also to what others need. We may or may not be healing witches, but healing is often a power and one of the steps on the path to empowerment and the ability to breathe light into others and the world. I gave to others what I drew into myself, what I needed. My feelings, which had been deemed as too much in my childhood and at times in relationship to others, were also my guide. My internal untangling process taught me how to help others untangle, how to be with them in a place of patient love, like the sun warming the bud so it can open.

7
Weaving Together

The healing of ourselves as healers has to take place first. Bringing ourselves to wholeness, we become more sensitive to other people. In the change of consciousness that happens within us, we bring about change of consciousness in those around us and in the planet itself.
~ Marion Woodman

Walking My Path

Finally, I am walking on my walk,
just because it is mine.

Finally,
I am older, embedded in the middle of my years,
made sure, certain by time.

Finally,
I am slowing down and coming to a center.
I am shedding old skins.
I root like a tree.

Gratefully, I let go.
Each chaotic thought falls deep
over the edge
like water pounding
over the fall
crashing down onto rock
pressures and have tos flung
into the air
a million particles
of mist.

Layer after layer
drop away
like clothes to the floor
before the bath
like dandelion parachutes
released to the wind.

Finally,
I hear a sound and it is mine.
My sound, sweet sound,
above the din.

A road unwinds with each step,
each foot placed down
on the earth firmly roots.

My walk and I am singing on it.
I am singing to be out in the sun.
I am singing my sound and rejoicing.
I leave people and towns behind.
I walk to me.

The Parts of Me

1991. I am living in a loft, the Lower East Side of Manhattan. Bleeker and the Bowery. Across from the nightclub and famed venue of punk rock, CBGB. A friend refers me to a healer. Jess. She uses a healing method that works with subpersonalities and parts. Voice Dialogue. She instructs me to identify all the different parts of myself. She hands me two sheets of paper with twenty-six questions. I am to answer the questions on the paper for each part. I find seventeen aspects of myself. I explore each of these parts – and answer twenty-six questions for each one. This is a crucial part of deconstructing who I am so I can rebuild a solid self, a witch self who can stand on her own two feet.

The first part I find is the little anxious one – I need to feel safe. I am small, young. I leave my body and flutter to the ceiling when upset or scared. I came into being at the age of two. My talent is my sensitivity. I am on guard, alert to danger. I am afraid of violence and cruelty. I relate most to Bill. Bill is the part of myself who protects me. He is strong and more able to stand up to others. He provides some solidity to my being.

As I answer the questions, I understand this part of me better. I see this part clearly. What is a messy merge begins to delineate, like the crisp edges of sun peeping around a cloud.

In my work with clients, we sometimes identify their parts. Despair. Jealousy. The Fuck You. The Responsible One. The Protector. The Spiritual One. The Sad Child. We look at how they relate to each other, the traumas or stresses they were created under.

The roles they play in negotiating with reality and survival. The damage they do in that person's life and relationships due to their rigidity.

Parts Does Not Equal Disorder

I do not have dissociative identity disorder. This is simply a way of looking at the structure of the personality. While I have parts (we all do), each part is easily accessible. The central I can see them all. They are not living separate lives unbeknownst to me. Each of us is made of many selves and parts. Richard C. Schwartz, Ph.D., who founded Internal Family Systems, developed a therapeutic system around this concept – helping people heal by identifying and listening to their parts. Although I do not know about Dr. Schwartz's work until many years later.

I continue with my self-work, reading and engaging with several of Lucia Capacchione's books, such as *The Creative Journal*, *Recovery of Your Inner Child*, and more. I read *Voice Dialogue* by Hal and Sidra Stone. I do this work before I begin any significant therapy. It is work that allows me to begin to restructure my relationship with myself. Later, I will do work that will help me restructure my relationships with others. I am on my path.

Developing a Witness

1997. I sit with my therapist, Kelly. We are upstairs above her house in her office. She has short gray hair and intense eyes. She is older, perhaps my mother's age. I find her intimidating. She seems so solid, so in charge, so unafraid. I am talking, rolling over the surface of my life, what happened when.

Fast. Anxious. She slowly draws me into the deeper feelings under my racing thoughts.

One day, I am talking and then I hear her voice. "Where have you gone?" she asks. Gone? What does she mean? I realize I have spaced out, left the room. I am becoming more aware of myself moment to moment. I am developing an internal witness.

Several years into my work with Kelly, I realize that I deeply enjoy this process. I begin to consider becoming a therapist. I go back to school to finish my bachelor's degree, and then in 1999, I begin my graduate work. Kelly is involved in GTILA, The Gestalt Therapy Institute of Los Angeles, and encourages me to get advanced training in Gestalt Therapy. In 2003, I begin Relational Gestalt Training at The Pacific Gestalt Institute, a subset of GTILA. I love this training. We spend one weekend a month learning Gestalt theory, role-playing, practicing. Gestalt theory is complex. It is based on principles of Eastern philosophy and works closely with present-moment awareness. Relational Gestalt Therapy's focus strongly includes the relationship between the therapist and the client. This is not the Freudian approach of the therapist being a blank screen. Instead, the therapist uses her person when working with a client. This is new for me. I am used to hiding myself, staying insular, not showing my reactions and feelings. Now, I am using them to help guide the therapy. I continue this training for four years.

※

Learning to Relate

2006. One of our Gestalt training weekends. I sit across from Susan with the group around us watching. We call this a fishbowl. I am the therapist, and she is the client in this role-play. We role-play to practice and develop our relational therapy skills, to teach, and discuss what we saw happen, what it brought up for us, what we learned, what could have been done differently.

Susan is telling me about an event with her mother. She is sad. I tell her I feel sad as I listen to her. She tears up. We are eye to eye, heart to heart connecting. We continue this way, connecting, mirroring. I stay close to her feeling self and close to my feeling self. This is new, so different from how I learned to be in my family. She feels held. She feels seen. This is healing for her. It is life-changing for me to stop hiding, to show my vulnerabilities, to use my feelings to connect to someone else. I am now deep in relational work. I am deep in understanding a new way to relate, a new way to heal.

Finding My Feet

It is 2003. I am sitting with two older men, David and Jim. They are interviewing me to see if they will accept me into their training center. I want to learn what they are teaching. Intersubjectivity. How there is no true objectivity. How who we are alters the other person and vice versa. Like colors. How red next to yellow looks different than red next to blue. The same red color side by side, but looking completely different in relationship to another color.

I also want to build a practice near their location in the Brentwood/West LA area. We talk. They ask questions. David does not make eye contact with me the entire time we are together. He is looking at the ceiling. As the interview ends and I am about to leave, I shoot a question at him. "Why haven't you made eye contact with me? What are you avoiding?" He looks at me and explains that he can think better without eye contact. My last questions ensure my entry into this program. They are looking for people who can step outside the "box." People who can challenge the status quo. People who are willing to rock the boat. I do not yet know I have this capacity. Or that the pressures of this training will force me to develop it.

I begin training at the center, located in Los Angeles. This training and three other training sites I attended over five years will accrue hours towards the more than 3,000 hours of working with people, supervision, education, and training needed to sit for the licensing exams. The training is rigorous and is a two-year commitment. I see ten or more clients a week here and more at the other training sites. I have two one-hour individual supervision sessions a week. I am part of group supervision for several hours a week. I am part of an educational group and a process group.

Process Group

The process group is intense. It is a Tavistock-style group, meaning that the leader is hands-off. Anything goes. The group members are in charge of themselves, and nobody knows what anybody will do or what will happen.

David is the "leader." He sits and allows whatever happens to occur. Once in a while, he may interject with a question.

The group includes people from the previous year and then us, the trainees who have just joined. The group is scary to me. There are eight of us. Of the prior year's members, three of the trainees have a hatred for the fourth member, which has carried forward into my first year there. I watch them bully her, put her down, spew hatred towards her. I am horrified. These are young people with advanced degrees who have chosen a profession of helping others heal. Why is this allowed to happen? Why hasn't David put a stop to it? I am steeped in fear, but I cannot watch what is occurring without getting involved.

Some of us begin to challenge what is happening. We begin to alter the group dynamics. There are moments in this group where I step into my power.

One day, Brian, a group member in his second year, tells me I am angry. Who does he think he is to tell me what I am feeling? And him, stilted in the area of feeling himself. I think he is full of shit, and his saying that makes me angry. He does not know what I am feeling. I hit the table between us full force. The lamp jumps. Brian jumps. Everyone jumps. "I grew up with anger. This is what anger looks like. Don't tell me what I am feeling." I do not know where this impulse has come from. It flows through me. It is effective.

Another day, one of the three friends who had bullied the fourth member of the group began to verbally attack Joyce. Joyce is in my year. I am sitting next to her. I feel her leave her body and float to the ceiling. I am terrified but cannot watch this happen. I take her hand and tell her to breathe with me. We breathe together. She returns to her body.

The three friends are mortified. They want to be healers. They can now see what healing is. I am the mirror showing them who they are, who they have not yet decided to become. There is a story about African elephants – the young males have no older elephants to discipline and teach them. They become destructive elephants who terrorize. Older elephants are introduced to their territory. They are taught how to behave by the older and wiser elephants. The destructive young elephants change. They become socialized and relational.

Group Supervision

Our group supervision is led by Melissa. The goal of this group is to help us break down our defenses, see deeper into who we are, how we operate, how we protect ourselves. So that, in turn, we can see our clients' defensive structure more clearly. She works with one of us individually in front of the group each week. She has a knack for pulling the rug out from under us. What she says, does, her method, I do not fully understand. I only know each of us becomes disoriented, vulnerable, teary, unsure. It is a skill. I find it traumatic. I need support, not what she offers. I resist her. She does not like that. She wants me to take what she has to offer, but to me, it feels like submitting to a rape. I will not do it. She tells me she offered me this glorious buffet, but I will not eat anything. I tell her it is her buffet, not mine.

Melissa does not understand collaboration unless she is in charge. She does not understand co-creative healing. I stand in her blind spot, and she in mine. Due to the stresses of this training, I have started with a new therapist, a supervisor, and trainer at the Pacific Gestalt Institute.

Sylvia helps me find my ground, my power, my right to show myself, to be who I am. I am beginning to change. I am starting to find my voice and my feet. I am beginning to see that I am not weak and scared. I am beginning to see who I am. I am beginning to find more of my witch self.

Path

The path appears as we conjure it. We make the path; the path makes us. A witch does not develop only alone. The intrapsychic (what is within, the components that make up the self) and the interpersonal (what is between ourselves and others) are firmly wrapped around each other. The work I did by myself, the sorting of who I was, was with parts of myself that had developed in relational contexts. The later interpersonal work I did also impacted who I was inside. There is no inside and outside. Everything is relational. Nothing lives in isolation.

A witch needs others to fully understand herself. Others who struggle with the same issues. Others who have talents they are growing, developing, sharpening. I was lucky to have met others who would affirm me, help me see myself, and I would do the same for them. Others who had witchy pieces and an interest in the mysteries of healing. Together, we knit and weave. We support and teach each other. We share and heal. We develop and co-create. And yet, it is our individual commitment to our journey that impels us.

8
HONORING SPIRIT

...The impermanence of the body should give us great clarity, deepening the wonder in our senses and eyes . Of this mysterious existence we share and are surely just traveling through...
~ Hafiz

※

Animating Force

There are mountains in the distance – the Olympic Mountain range. It has snow on its peaks and is shrouded in clouds. As I notice my body, my breathing, this present moment, I feel its presence. It's being-ness. This mountain range is one of the guardians of the island where I live. My moment-to-moment awareness, my mindfulness have allowed me to be tuned into this knowing. This is an aspect of my healing, being more deeply grounded in my body, in my awareness. I am not lost in fractured thought, anxiety, worry, or depression. I am here.

Within each of us is an animating force. The vital essence that gives us our life spark.

No matter what is occurring, who or what we are, it is there. It may be clouded with dark thoughts, fears, bad habits. But still, it is there. Some say it is the breath of god.

Attunement

The divine feminine, also known as the Shechinah, comes from the Hebrew word meaning presence, dwelling, or settling and denotes the dwelling of the holy presence of god in embodied existence. While the divine masculine historically resides "out there," the divine feminine resides "in here." Wiccan belief worships nature and often sees spirit as Mother Earth and Father Sky, reinforcing the idea of the feminine embodied in form and the masculine more as thought and action.

The divine feminine is the life imbued in form. Without that life force, our bodies die, decay, return to the body of the earth. As witches, we are attuned to the divine feminine. We are attuned to the cycles of nature, to the god or spirit within form. Spirit offers us an entryway into meaning, into the root of who we each are. Spirit points to what we cannot see but are aware of and can feel. I feel connected to the spirits of the beings around me. I feel the presence of the mountains, the tree, the crow, the osprey, the kingfisher, and the cloud.

Attunement to spirit enlarges us. It means we have the capacity to honor each other, the deeper other, not the surface form. It means we move out of primarily relating to the external, the material and develop a relationship with the inner, the interior, the light of the soul. It means we look into the eyes of another being and see a potential relationship, a connection.

My attunement to spirit has enabled me to see beyond our visible and more exterior concerns to innate relationships and dynamics.

I remember, as a child, knowing not everything I was told, saw, or read was the truth.

I knew that holding a degree of skepticism was healthy for me. I wanted to decide what I thought about a piece of information, not just accept it. I was already setting myself up to trust my own knowing rather than believing what others thought I should believe. I was honoring the truth of spirit above what others assumed.

I Knew

Our family moved from suburban New Jersey to rural Pennsylvania when I was eight. I started third grade at my new school, in a land of farmers and fundamental religion. A land with fields of corn, soybeans, and cows. Billboards on country roads yelled out, "Accept Jesus or burn in hell forever." Sometime during that first year of school there, somebody asked me if I had been baptized. I said no. A group of children began taunting me, saying that I would go to hell.

I was amazed they believed that. My need to see clearly was stronger than my need to merge and join. Even as a child, I knew that heaven and hell were not holding areas waiting for good and evil, not lined up with morality, but were more internal places, reflecting states of being, states of consciousness. I also knew whether I was baptized or not had nothing to do with how my life would unfold and whether I was blessed or cursed.

I somehow recognized and saw beyond the structure of human religious belief systems. Probably because both of my parents were religious outliers. I did not believe anyone could be condemned by human laws when a good portion of humanity fell outside those definitions and when spiritual truths were higher, more powerful laws.

Gateway

Honoring spirit is a gateway to connection, to love, to dancing with the unfolding of the self, the planet, the universe. Spirit also lets us know we are just one part of the web of life, part of the I-thou relationship with all of life. It allows a reorientation from being the center of the universe to being an essential piece of the multiplicity of the universe. To being part of the murmuration of birds as they shift and change formation, moving across the sky. Honoring spirit means becoming truly relational and, at times, blending energies with others for the greater good. It is moving from I to we.

✷

Alive

Cold reddened cheeks
I stand among the trees
waiting.

Soft feathers
the sound of chickadee de de de
trilling through the air.

Patience is my tool.
Trust is my talent.
Will you be my friend?
Take me worlds away.

Let me find
myself anew.

✹

Enliven

The winter I was eleven years old, I decided to tame the birds coming to the feeder I put up. I would stand near the feeder, watch the nuthatches and chickadees grab a seed, and fly off with it. I started a distance from the feeder. Each day, I moved in closer. Eventually, I was right under the feeder. The little birds became familiar with me. One day, I put some seeds in my palm and held my hand out. It took a few days, but eventually, a chickadee landed on my hand; its tiny feet clutched my finger. I could feel its minuscule weight. I stopped breathing for that moment, holding perfectly still, my heart beating wildly, filled with happiness. It felt like such a huge accomplishment that this little being was unafraid of me.

This was my way of connecting with the bird spirits and their realm – the realm of the outdoors and wilderness, of wild creatures, of the non-human world. It was a way I could be part of the natural world and have contact with wild beings without strife or fear.

That moment of feeling those little feet clutching my finger expanded my world beyond my family, beyond my mother's inability to connect emotionally, beyond my father's rages. I experienced a similar feeling when I rode my horse Specks through snow-covered fields, the snow so high he bounded in great leaps. The ice-covered branches sparkling in the sun. I was in my magical realm and out of the house with its ghosts and demons.

Specks made me powerful as we galloped over the hills. I was a part of him. An extension of him. We trusted each other.

We were so connected we communicated without the control of saddle or bridle. Isn't that the connection we all want? Connection and hearing each other, flying together, adjusting to each other, enlarging each other's lives. Control isn't part of this. Love and appreciation are.

We are never only in one world, one dimension. Often, there is a predominant world, perhaps the world of family or work. But there is always more we can reach into. It may be art, ideas, nature, spirits. It doesn't matter. While one reality may be crushing, there may be another within our reach which is enlivening.

Love Line

It is my first time taking mushrooms.
We mix them with honey.
Ingest.
Wait.

I am with my brother
outside, Oak
trees, golden grass, sky.

First, the world breaks
into patterned motifs
from another time and place.

And then,
I feel a line of love arcing
from my heart across the land
like a rainbow.

I feel it reach, connect to the heart of my partner.

We have been struggling.
And yet,
I bloom, heart expanded, alive.

This relationship will end.
The love line will stay.

Honoring

Sometimes, we meet the right person at the wrong time. Paul was my third boyfriend. We were together for about two years. I broke up with him roughly ten years before my first marriage. I needed more experiences, more disappointments, and more lessons before I would be ready to commit to working through the difficulties of a long-term relationship.

❉

Letter to Paul

Dear Paul,
I have thought about you throughout the years. More than anybody else I've had a romantic relationship with.

I'm happily married now to someone I love deeply, to someone I consider "the one," but you still float through my mind. Not as someone I want to be with, but as someone I loved and walked away from without fully honoring who you were. I wish I had been more mature. I wish I had been there for you more completely. I wish I had appreciated you more fully. I wish I had fought harder to work through our difficulties.

I wish I had been able to communicate and tell you how much you meant to me. I still think of when you would take a bath, and I would sit down next to the bathtub, and we would talk. Those times felt special to me.

Intimate and close. You were fun and creative. Playful. Serious. Different.

I don't know if you are still on the planet. I haven't been able to find you. Maybe we would have nothing in common now. But I wish I had honored you, and I wish you to know that. We spent a few years together… as we do with many.

And those times are precious. Sometimes, they end and pass by without having ever been consciously honored.

I know you had significant issues. I remember when you told me, sobbing, that your father used to beat you up. I know you got caught up in cocaine. I know about that woman at your job who was trying to seduce you while we lived together and perhaps succeeded. She flirted with you in front of me, in our home. You liked the attention, even though you loved me.

After I had moved to NYC, at some point, we talked on the phone, and you were dating that co-worker who had tried to seduce you while we were still together. I didn't know what to say. Didn't understand what you were trying to tell me. I was mute.

I could hear you missing me even as you told me about your life, your career, and struggles. I didn't know how to reach out and comfort.

It seemed you wanted that. I just know when you hung up, I felt empty and alone.

You were a dear and lovely being. And I didn't have any idea of how to be in a relationship. When the conflicts came up and the in-love feeling left, some part of me was out. I needed love so badly I couldn't tolerate the difficulties. That was on me.

I found it - the initial love that felt like a drug. Time and time again. The quick in-love fix. It took me years to learn how to have a long-term relationship that worked. I want you to know that. It wasn't just you. It was me. Me more than you. I had the bigger issue. I was the one who left.

After we broke up and were trying to be friends before I moved away, I fondly remember the times you took me out to eat in Chinatown.

I remember your kindness. I remember you telling me you loved me after it was too late. I had already fallen for someone else. Someone completely spellbinding and also completely unable to have a real relationship. Someone who did not love me like you. I know I caused you pain and suffering.

I am so sorry. I hope you know this in your heart, in your soul. Even if you have passed, I hope that somehow, these words, my intentions infuse you with love. I hope they reverberate through you, wrap around you, nourish you.

In some ways, I am the same person. I have the same sensitive soul. But I have grown. I have developed a voice that can speak. I am no longer mute. My journey has changed me. I am now able to stick through the difficult times. I am able to find out where I am triggered or caught, where the other is triggered. I am able to unknot the knots. To take what is damaged and make it whole. I could not do that when I was with you. I wasn't fully formed before. Nor were you. But we each had hearts, and my heart remembers yours.

I hope you found a true love, a long-term relationship, or marriage. I hope your life was or is happy. I hope you found someone perfect for you.

✺

DESIRE

Wish - await what the stars will bring.

Diminutive scrawny child
your black braids tight to your head
turquoise, yellow, and red
bow-shaped barrettes.

I send you my love
my hope,
sweet on a moonbeam.

May you be blessed.
May you be loved.
May you find happiness
and your heart's contentment.

✹

Child Abuse Report

She was seven years old. A wiry child. I just out of graduate school, was still being supervised. She was talkative and energetic. Always so happy to see me. She leans against me, holds my hand. She wants to be held, to sit on my lap. A little bird with an open mouth. Feed me.

She wants me to marry her father. She wants a mother again. Every time I see her, she begins her work on me, convincing me to marry her father. A natural sales child. I do not see anything wrong with her. Just a child growing up on a barren piece of earth, missing the nurturing of a mother, so hungry. So in need of nourishment.

She did not know where her mother was, what had happened to her. I did not know the story either, why she had left, where she was, if she lived. I suspected drug addiction. Her father sounded harsh, not nurturing. But I knew he loved her. He gave the school permission for her to see me. He wanted her to get whatever she needed to grow, to develop, to become.

You Are Not Bad

One day, she told me she visited her grandmother, and her grandmother had beaten her. Not a quick swat. I tell her she does not deserve to be hit. I tell her she is not bad.

This is not okay. I do not know what to do. I know the law. I must do a child abuse report. I do not want to. I am on the fence. I wish I could forget her words.

Innocent

Little girl
who I love,
you teach me.

I will
listen to my heart.

I will put fear away,
stuff it in a bag or box.

I will stand outside under the sun
and pray.

✷

Severed

I make the report. I call and ask the father to meet with me. He agrees, but he does not show. He tells his child she may not see me anymore. He tells the school to take her out of therapy. She is heartbroken. I am heartbroken. I cannot fix this. I do not know how. All of us caught in something massive, cold, and unable to feel.

It is not her father's fault. Who knows what injustices he has lived through, is living through? Who knows how our world, our system, people have betrayed him? Of course, he does not trust.

Child Protective Services has interviewed them. Nothing has changed except I cannot see this child anymore. Eventually, her father allows her into a group session I have with several kids. It is not the same. She gets to play, but the one-on-one time that nourishes her is no longer. Her family did not change. Her grandmother did not say, "I made a mistake to beat that child. My granddaughter is not bad; she just needs love."

I wish I had not made the report. It was a mistake. A stupid law that tries to put all interactions into legal boxes instead of trusting that the clinician can navigate and make the correct choice. An agency that does not have an intuition. Just reports. How can we do what is best when we cannot listen to our inner guidance. Lives do not fit into boxes. Situations are all different. Love is expressed differently, as is punishment.

Have To's

I was still sorting through fear and intuition at that time. I was not yet clear. My choices were not always influenced by a perspective higher than my own. Instead, I heard the "have to" of my licensing board.

Today, I would not make that report. I would claim I did not hear about any beatings. I would keep that child safe in a different way. Her environment did not change regardless of whether the report was made, but had I not made the report, she would have continued to be nourished every week when we were together.

I hope she is having a good life, not harsh like the one she was in when I knew her. I hope her father found her a loving mother. I hope her grandmother saw the errors of her ways. I hope she knew I truly cared. I am sorry. Sorry, sorry, sorry. I wanted to give you more.

✹

Projection

You.
You who think you know.
You who would judge me.

I stand tall. I see myself.

I push away your judgment.
I take your dark heart,
your ugly feelings and crooked thoughts,
give them back to you.

They are not mine.
Own them.

My power, my talents, my abilities
They are mine.

I stand tall. I see myself.
I dance.

Jyoti Singh Pandey

Sometimes, a story hits me hard. Sometimes, a person's journey breaks my heart, and I struggle to find what it means. I struggle to know there is meaning because how else do I keep my heart open? How else do I know the universe is good? How else do I know that there is a loving god?

In 2012 I read a news article about the rape and murder of Jyoti Singh Pandey. It scorched me to the core. Jyoti was a twenty-three-year-old physiotherapy intern who was beaten, gang-raped, and tortured with a metal bar by six men, essentially disemboweling her. Massive damage occurred to her intestines, which were partially pulled out, her uterus, and genitals. The attack happened in South Delhi, India. She died about two weeks later in a hospital. Jyoti came from a poor family whose father worked double shifts to pay for her schooling. Her attack precipitated worldwide protests and brought attention to violence against women and the skewed justice system in India.

I wrote the following piece for her.

For Jyoti

I remember when I first learned her name and saw her picture. She was smiling with warm brown eyes and long dark hair. She looked petite, young, and sweet. I was glad to learn her name. I was glad to see her picture. I was glad to get to know her a bit in this way.

Although I never knew her personally, along with many others, I felt enormous grief when I heard the story of what was done to her, of what became her murder.

My horror grew with each detail revealed. A horrific attack on one small female by six monsters – for who could call them men? A young woman maimed, torn, raped, and left for dead.

How do we survive these violations against spirit, against body and against life? When will we love others, our home the earth, in a truly respectful way? When will we live in a new world?

Standing Together

And yet, a world in grief stood up against this act. Why? Because we know what happened was as wrong as anything could ever be. Because we know women are beautiful, life is beautiful, and all deserve to be treated with love. Still, we are left with enormous grief – a grief so immense that we do not know what to do with it – and our own trauma – the trauma of powerlessness, the trauma of being a witness to horror.

How do we heal our grief? How do we mend ourselves? How do we recover?

It was only when I started to imagine her healing that I was able to tolerate the grief I felt. Only then could I somehow be with this event and be in my life without feeling shattered.

I imagine her delicate body ripped apart, abused, ruined, and bloodied. Metal against flesh, crimson red spilled, later the darkening of gangrene, spreading like ink sinking into paper. I imagine her pain.

I imagine her pure and innocent, barely an adult, stepped on and destroyed. Her body, like all our bodies, tender, fragile, easily trespassed.

I want all of us to notice the tender texture of the purple and yellow pansy, of the lily bud, of the rose. I want us to see the delicate and soft beauty of our skin, our eyes. Our bodies deserve love, whether human, animal, plant, the body of our earth.

I imagine her as a tiny baby, new and fresh, loved and held. Delicate fingers with their little fingernails – how we all start, precious and perfect. The happiness of her parents as they looked into her eyes, as they witnessed and engaged with her first smile. The years they spent nurturing her, caring for her. Her family will ache forever for the loss of this part of themselves.

I wish to take my hands and smooth her hair, make her comfortable. I wish to heal her wounds, her destroyed body, and erase the horror she lived through. I wish to erase her pain, her disappointment, the knowing that she would not live to see her dreams realized. The career she would not have. The people she would not help. The lives she would not touch. The family and friends she would never see again. The husband and children, grandchildren, nieces, and nephews she would never know.

Soft Flower Petals

I wish that she is out of pain and harm's way. I wish she is in a place of beauty, love, and light. May she be surrounded by love that feels like a thousand soft flower petals, caressing her spirit, healing the hatred and horror she had to endure.

May her spirit, the spirit that came through her warm brown eyes, feel safe and free.

I wish that from the vantage point of wherever she is, she can see that her life mattered, that she was precious, and that even her death has illuminated many. I wish that she knows what she went through is helping change the consciousness of others.

I wish she could have lived in a world where all are treated with caring, with respect, with reverence. I wish that she could have been safe. I wish this for everyone.

Blind

How does one destroy beauty – the beauty of our bodies, the beauty of our spirits? How can one be so blind, so lost, so depraved? Who are these men who do not cherish and protect what is young, vulnerable, and beautiful – who hate women, hate life itself? Who are these men with dark hearts of stone? Who are these men who stomp out beauty, who blame the innocent for their own vileness?

There are those who say she deserved it, that she is responsible, that womankind is dirty, that she asked for it. Do you not know that the feminine is one of the faces of god?

That beauty shines from our tender bodies? Do you not see god in each of us?

You are the small-minded ones. You are lost, you who cannot see straight, for where there is beauty, you see ugliness, and you blame. You are the ones who believe women are less and wish to possess and control. And who are we as a species that we've tolerated these people who cannot honor others? Why have we not put an end to this yet?

I am done with you. I am done with excuses. I am done with your sickness. I am done with your crooked thinking and your making of rules and structures that do not serve our spirits. Your darkness will not be tolerated. No longer will you get away with treating life without love. Run, for you are on the way out. The tide is turning. You will be pummeled by the new consciousness. You will be cut by the teeth of our outrage. You will be washed away. You are obsolete.

Free

Jyoti lived her life as she wished. She stood in integrity. She did not worry that the world could not, would not honor her. She lived with the freedom she desired despite what it would cost her. Some part of her was free, was unwilling to be bound by the debris of others. Some part of her knew that living her truth was more important than repressing her spirit, despite the price. She lived her truth, and her death cast a light revealing those who hide from light and truth.

Demand

I am glad I can feel. I am glad for those of us who choose to feel our outrage, our grief, and our despair. I am glad we can feel horror and pain. I am glad this event injured me. Who would we be if it did not? Who would we be if we lived in our heads, among old defective ideas, rationalizing, justifying, blaming, and devaluing? It is through feeling our connection to others that we can honor who they are, their spirit.

I expect to walk through this world safe, honored, loved. I have this right. I demand it, not just for me but also for everyone. I demand it because my demand changes what is. My demand awakens possibility. My demand permeates and rings through the universe.

I remember a conversation with my father when I was younger. I did not believe in the death penalty. He did. I disagreed with him. I told him that anybody could be rehabilitated – it was just a matter of time, and effort, energy, and love. I no longer believe it is that simple. Sometimes, the rehabilitation needed will take lifetimes and experiences of suffering to change the mind and open the soul. I was young and naïve, and I did not want to believe that there were those so ruined that hope was a dim light shining a universe away. I did not wish to believe in evil. I wish it were not so. I wish each of us carried only kindness in our hearts. I wish the world's beauty was celebrated and any acts that sullied Jyoti Singh Pandey were removed.

She spoke for all of us. Both the beauty of her spirit and her annihilation. Her body is also our body. Her pain is ours. Her body is the body of the earth.

Our female bodies are like Mother Earth; we feed and nurture others. Like Mother Earth, it is the bounty of our bodies that allows life to continue and the bounty of our love that enables others to grow. We are to be celebrated, not scorned. We are to be honored and cherished. Perhaps Jyoti did not die in vain. Perhaps her suffering was not for naught. Perhaps she is a light showing us the path.

✹

Sacred Beings

Cathedral of trees standing.
Ancient forest presence.
Guardians.
Holders of space.

Earth mountains rock crystal
rooted
reaching deep.

Air swaying
breeze fresh clear.

Fire sun heat
activating, molecules dancing.

Water moisture rain river
wet, lubricating.

Spirit illuminating
vibration, angelic.

My friends.
I
feel awe,
honor
your divinity.

Communion

Sometime between 2011 and 2014, my husband Mike and I drove through the redwoods on one of our trips from Southern California to Washington State.

We left the hot, dusty inland freeway and headed west toward the coast. As we drove, we entered a tunnel of trees. They pulled us in and surrounded us while they reached upward, a cathedral of beings. I could feel the spirit, the beauty, the health of this forest of beings. Verdant ferns in patches of bright green at the foot of tall reaching shafts of dark bark. Up, up, a community with its own meaning. I had stepped into their world, a small visitor traveling through the winding road at the bottom of these sacred giants.

There are some things that you can just feel. That is how you know what they are. Like stepping into an empty church and feeling the vast and peaceful energy. It is a privilege to step into another's world, to experience their grace and beauty. I felt lucky to do so.

Family

Under the trees are the roots. A community of roots nourished by a community of fungi – the mycorrhizae. These unseen beings support the community of trees. I love how each tree stands tall, reaches up to the sky, a heroic quest, while the roots entwine and are supported by an interconnected community below. Isn't this how it is with humans? Don't we rise up and grow because of the interconnections with and support of others? Are we so full of hubris that we cannot see that we are all a family?

I do not believe I could be here on earth if there were not beauty, if aspects of life were not like a cathedral with the feeling of awe, love, truth, or perhaps even god. I could not be here if I thought that what was here is all that is possible. I need to know that there is more. That it is possible to create more. Perhaps what I envision will not occur for a millennium, long after I am dust, but it is the possibility that feeds me.

Worlds Within Worlds

My husband told me a story of when he rescued a dragonfly. It was trapped in his house. He managed to get it out. Later, sitting in the hot tub, that same dragonfly, fluorescent copper, came and visited. From the outside, it was just another insect. But my husband felt its gratitude. He experienced a communion with this being.

If we could see inside each of us, we would see a universe that is vast. Yet, from the outside, there is just a person, an animal, an insect, or a tree. Inside is a universe as large, as complex, as beautiful as our own galaxy full of stars, every expanding, moving. We are worlds within worlds. Are we aware of this? It is our awareness that empowers us, that allows us to see the spirit of others. With every in-breath and out-breath, a universe moves through me, changed by me. Do we know how big we are, how big it all is, how rich? Do we forget, or are we simply blind? With every act we take, we alter our world. The forests we chop down, the beings we eat, the music we make, the love we spread. It is through our awareness that we can make each action we take positive and recognize the incredible power that we have.

Gratitude

Yesterday, I ate a Dungeness crab for lunch. He was large. I imagined him as a granddaddy crab, an older, bigger, and perhaps wiser crab than most. As I pulled him apart, taking his top shell off and cleaning out what used to be his insides, I was very aware of him as a fellow creature. He had a face, body, and legs. He had had a life. I felt a sense of gratitude towards him for sacrificing his life for me. When we buy "meat" in the grocery store, it is easy to miss that it came from another being. The problem is less with the eating of this "meat" and more with the disconnection from recognizing that another being made a sacrifice of his or her life for me. As well as making sure that those who are sacrificed for us – and not of their own choosing – have a life worth living while they are here. When I feel the sacrifice made, I am in touch with and more able to honor the spirit of others.

Web of Connection

For a long time, I have believed in the concept of guidance. I get messages, am directed in specific directions, and sometimes just know things. I am aware that an unseen community is also supporting me and all of us. I am ever grateful for this support. It is the not knowing and acknowledging the web of support and interconnection that is the core of one of the biggest problems that we have… the idea that we are alone, that we are not part of or responsible for the well-being of our entire community.

A while ago, as I was meditating, I was not happy about the noise from a leaf blower interfering with my peace.

Then, as I shifted my thoughts to the man who had to spend part of his day in the middle of that noise to survive, I felt myself loosen a little.

I felt more compassion. It is not just about me. Yet the designers of such machines are focused on getting the job done, not on the experience of the people who operate these machines or those who must listen to them. This limited point of view creates enormous problems in our world in many scenarios. A more expansive awareness of the inner space and needs of all, coupled with compassion, would cause us to end much of the suffering on this planet.

All of life has spirit and soul. It really is that simple. Sure, they have different forms, different capacities, but I can hear them. See their spirits. Learn from them. Bond with them. Honor them.

This is a door I wish humanity would open more fully. To see the value of those who are not in human form. To see the magic of other beings. To help them. To consider them in our decisions. To share our world rather than relegate them to the parts we do not want.

Freedom

We live in a world of enormous possibilities. One of our freedoms is the freedom to think and imagine, as well as the freedom to look at ourselves and apply our thoughts, dreams, and imaginings.

Recently, reading, I came across the idea that the four elements – Water, Air, Earth, and Fire –are conscious beings.

Although I am somewhat familiar with the Indigenous Peoples' ceremony of giving thanks to the four directions as beings, I had never really thought about it like this.

These four spiritual and archetypal beings – meaning beings at the root of our consciousness and the structure of our world - hold space for us to live in this physical reality. This is somewhat similar to seeing humanity as vast beings holding space for the multitudes of microbes within us. If the fabric of our very world and being is alive and conscious with intention, then that changes how we relate to our lives. We are held by others. And we hold others.

As I pondered upon this idea, I could feel the grace in it. Suddenly, everything was alive. Everything was conscious. There is meaning and intention in everything. I carried this idea with me. It comforted me somehow.

Seven Generations

A few days later, in a conversation, I mentioned the idea of making only decisions that would be good for those living seven generations from now – another idea from the Indigenous Peoples. I would extend this idea to what is good for all of us, not just the human species. An idea that if taken seriously, would completely reform our world. Every action would be contemplated as part of a web of intention, leading to specific wanted or unwanted results – to our co-created future.

If those four elements are conscious and alive, holding space for me, can I hold space for those who follow me? What choices will I make? Which ones will I change?

The pressures of our world dictate choices for living quick and easy. Fast food, fast lives, decisions to make a buck today. When did we fall away from life as sacred?

I notice how I am focused. I notice when I feel the aliveness of the mountains, the mist, the sun, the sky.

Support of Friends

Awareness and support. These are key. Of the non-human realms as well as the human realm. It is with the support of others that we can move deeper into our learning and development. Our journey of consciousness and awakening. These others, collaborators on our paths, include my friends. We guide each other, support each other, are channels for the divine for each other.

Beginning in 2003 and through 2007, I am taking advanced Gestalt training. I make friends with these other budding therapists in my training. We learn from each other, our practicing and interacting create a weave of healing and support. We collaborate, connect, tune into each other. We learn to be inclusive and harmonize, helping each member of our training group to grow. For example, in one of our Gestalt training groups, we had a new member who had just immigrated to the United States. She was full of fear but trying to prove herself. In the process, she pushed us all away. We wanted to get rid of her.

Our supervisor, Matthew, helped us support her, provide her with what she needed to integrate into our group, and step into the work we were doing rather than disrupt us. Instead of seeing her as a problem, a distraction from what we were doing, supporting her became part of our work as a group.

We adjusted to what was required instead of holding onto what we thought should be happening.

2006. I am sitting with Mikaela, whom I met at my first internship, for breakfast in a diner. We are talking, discussing, animated. We do peer supervision, meeting weekly to discuss how we work, what we are learning, to support each other with what is challenging. She and her daughter Debbie are members of my SoulCollage® group. Later, after I moved to San Diego, I often stayed with Mikaela on my nights in Los Angeles, squeezing in a morning walk with her where we talk. She joins a writing group with me. She invites me to a supervision group she is in. It is a rich cauldron of sharing and collaboration.

I met Shelly at a training center for intersubjectivity. She came in the year after me. I watch her in process group, watch her struggle to express what she is perceiving. Her ability to intuit and feel astonishes me. I want to know her. I want to learn more about who she is. I do. I see her talents and what she is working to overcome. We continue our relationship after our training ends, continue to nourish each other. These are healing witches, and knowing them affirms who I am.

I have other friends, other beings who are part of the web of my life, part of the web of support and awakening. Each enriches me as I enrich them.

While we are each on our own journey of becoming, we do it with the support of compassionate others. We teach each other, care for each other, listen to and tend each other. We create a fabric that holds not only ourselves but the people we serve. We create community and love. We bring light to ourselves and what we touch.

Your Aliveness

How are you focused on your life? Do you feel the aliveness in the mountains? In the mist, the sun, the sky? When you eat an apple, do you feel the crunch, smell the aroma, taste the sweet sourness? Do you feel the energy of the apple flow through you? Do you think about how you impact not just the now but also the future in each moment and every choice you make? This is an expansive place to stand, and it is hard to shrink it down to each choice in each moment. Yet, it is worthy of consideration. What would we change? How would we feel differently? What would we honor?

Would you remember you stand within the consciousness and bodies of others: The four sacred beings? The Water, The Air, The Earth, and The Fire? Would you remember your responsibility to them, your gratitude to them? Would you remember that despite your smallness in comparison, you have the entire cosmos within you as well? Would you see the sacredness we reside within, the sacredness residing within us?

It is easy to forget about the trees. Easy to forget about these other worlds. For there are so many different worlds. We tend to fall into our own insular routine. It is in honoring our connection with others we genuinely become whole and spiritual.

This energy is spiritual in nature. It is of the heart, love, and the Anahata chakra – represented by a twelve-petaled lotus and two intersecting triangles, symbolizing the union of masculine and feminine and the entryway to god.

I do my best to remember there is so much more than me. To know that each and every one of us has a perspective and a place.

The trees, the four sacred beings, the beings I share this earth with.

Like how the mycorrhizae support the trees, relationships and connection are at the root of everything. Relationship to self, to others, to the world. When we stop and take notice of others with respect or honor, of their beauty, joy, or suffering, we expand our world.

My awareness fluctuates. Moves to different places. I do not always hold an expansive awareness. Yet, sometimes, I do. I may not yet be aware enough to consistently hold how I am impacting not just my now but also the future in each moment and every choice I make. Yet to do so puts me in the center of a powerful place. Possibility radiates as each of us steps into this way of being. Into awareness of the web of interconnection, the spirit in everything, and our power to transform.

✷

Celestial Movement

My sister has photographed
the green flash
as the sun dips
just below
the long lean stretch
of horizon.

The increase of light
as the golden orb
disappears.

The earth turns
away
and towards again
a steady cycle
a celestial movement.

The orb
is always there.

And
shares its light
regardless.

Increasing Light

As a teenager, I used to sit among the pine trees on the hill behind our house. It was peaceful, the needled branches rustling in a bit of wind, sometimes the sounds of the chickadee and nuthatch filling the space. I wasn't fully present to that moment. Instead, I carried my worried and fearful self there. I worried about the problems of the world, the garbage we created, the lives that suffered. I worried about how I would navigate through the world, who I was supposed to be.

I used to ask myself, how do I save this struggling world? Now, I focus on creating what good I can bring into being within and around me. Using my magic to transmute what I can. Opening my mind and heart. Organizing what is in chaos into flow. Moving into acceptance. Into knowing there is a larger play happening here, even if I cannot see it.

My Heart

I think of Stumpy, the little dwarf white deer I feed. Early one morning, I am sitting with Stumpy. The birds are rustling, singing. I hear the *whuf, whuf, whuf* of a raven or hawk winging by. The air is fresh morning air. Stumpy's lips are warm on the palm of my hand as he carefully gathers the food pellets into his mouth. I hear them crunch, see his throat move as he swallows. I look up; his damp black nose is an inch from my face. He is observing me. Perhaps wondering who this being is who provides him with snacks.

When Stumpy came along, he pulled at my heart. If he were a human, he might be a dwarf. He isn't shaped quite right.

His legs are short, his body truncated. I first met Stumpy when his mother, now called MamaMama, was eating apples under the apple tree last fall. Beside her was a mini white being, Stumpy. I walked over and rolled some apples towards them.

I kept an eye on Stumpy after that and, in the winter, began to feed him. Stumpy eats carrots and apples out of my hands. His sweet, soft lips brush against my fingers as he takes treats. I feel his joy. He makes me smile.

Shared Prosperity

Stumpy is part of my world, and I have decided to join his world, to come closer rather than watch from a distance through the window, a world away. This is our generosity and our wisdom. To move from eking out survival to a shared prosperity. I watch him gallop across the yard in joy. I resonate. His joy, my joy.

Several years ago, there was another dwarf white deer. I noticed her after it was too late. I brought her an apple, rolled it across the ground to her. She was too sick to eat. I found her body a few days later.

I could have ignored Stumpy, not connected, let him live his separate life, watch him through the windows, but not intervene. I decide to intervene. Let him have food and enjoy more health. Let him not sicken and starve through the winter.

Even if life at times seems unkind, even if we get lost, lose our bearings, we can be kind. It is what we do to help those around us. We feel their plight. We want to connect. We want to give.

We want them to have as much joy as we do, as little suffering as possible. We want others to flourish because we see ourselves in them; we know ourselves to be them.

Gaia

Mother Earth is our world. I open the window to her. To a relationship with that which is around me, that which runs through me, that which I am embedded in.

I see her in the mists as they move over the mountains. I see her in the dew drops on the winter berries, glassy, reflecting land and sky, hit with a sparkle of sun. I see her in the cry of the black oystercatchers as they fly, haunting me with their call. I see her in the wind, the trees waving, shaking, sometimes shattering. I see her everywhere because I am a part of her, and everything I can experience with my senses is her.

I taste her when I bite into a peach. I feel the softness give way to my teeth, see the orange and yellow, smell the aroma. She is everywhere.

When I open my heart to Mother Earth, I feel not just magnificence but pain. When I look at patterns over time, I know she is changing. I know all of us who live within her embrace are part of this change.

Flow of Grace

Last year, there were many Bufflehead Ducks in Puget Sound in front of my office window. This year, there are almost none. I see the wounding around me. The loss of other creatures, other beings.

I am one person. My task in this life has been unraveling my wounds. Learning to live in the flow of grace. Teaching myself and others love.

Empowering the feminine, feminine knowing, feminine feelings. Vulnerability, reciprocity, love, caring.

I learn more about unconditional love. Sometimes it hurts. Like when someone you love says something mean or misunderstands you.

Loving Anyway

What is there to do, to change? Nothing. There is only the bruised self that chooses to continue to love because that is what it does, because that is the best action in the circumstances. Because to walk away, while easier, does not bring more tenderness to the planet.

We come to the planet not for ease but to increase love, to increase clarity despite limitations. Who do we hurt? The planet itself? Ourselves? Each other?

I am but one small molecule, one cell of this great breathing sphere.

I cannot hold our planet in my hands, but I can hold her in my mind. And in my heart. I know that I live within the abundance of her body. I feel her breathe as the trees breathe. I feel her in the darkness of night, in the sound of my heart beating, in the rush of air in and out of my lungs. I feel her when I walk down a dark wooded road alone, the moon a tiny crescent. The air crisp. The blood coursing through my body, the sound of the crunch of the gravel under my feet.

I tell our earth that I love her. I appreciate her moment by moment. I release the parts of me that hold energy and ways of being that do not help. I look at my life.

What do I need to change? Where do I take too much for granted? Where am I in harmony, and where am I out of sync?

Shifting the Tide

I am but one small person. But I can see the truth. I can see the disconnection. I can see through our deceit about what our home is, what we need, who we are.

My power over what is happening is limited. It will take many of us to shift the tide. Many who live in their hearts, who have wisdom and perspective, who love the body of this earth, which is also our bodies.

I choose to stand in the flow of light. I unravel the tangles so the light can flow through and bounce off. I have this power. We have this power.

Peace

Not all cures
are quick like
the sweet, sticky syrup
filling the spoon.

If I were a tree
a sapling perhaps
small but reaching
with visions large

would I know
the concentric growth rings
expanding outward
one by one
year by year
the path to becoming
the large spreading oak
on the hill?

Would I imagine
how each moment
came and went
the dew, breeze
the seasons turning
the heat and chill?

Would I realize
the patient road
to peace?

Together

I have moved deeper into my heart over the last decade. I am much stronger and have learned to hold boundaries and not be swayed by other's needs in the same way. Despite this, I am sensitive to those around me. My stronger and more boundaried self did not lose her heart and sensitivity. We can be both – boundaried and sensitive.

Today, in 2020, as the smoke from the fires begins to subside, a group of deer waits under the apple trees for apples to fall. There is not much food for them at this time of the year, the fall, and they rely on the apples to help them survive the upcoming winter.

I feel bad for the deer. I feel as if Calcutta is here in Washington state, where I live, where the lack of predators and concurrent overpopulation causes throngs of undernourished deer to congregate. There are five of them scattered across our large yard, the sky white with haze, fog, and the residue of smoke. The sun, a strange dark orange orb.

Generosity

When I prepare dinner, I take the vegetable scraps and throw them outside for the deer. I know it won't save them, but I want the deer to have a moment of pleasure in what seems to be a dull and hungry day, looking for almost non-existent food. I have neighbors who would rather throw their kitchen scraps away than encourage our deer problem, but I see it differently.

The deer problem comes from a lack of predators and not from a few measly bits of kitchen scraps. So, I stay in my heart and out of my head and offer them the bits I do not want, as well as trimmings from the garden.

I give what I can while also considering consequences and boundaries. I consider what is in my best interest. I consider what is in the best interest of all.

We come to this earth and do our best, but so many of us are beset by challenges that can be overwhelming. How do we get through these? Yes, in part by our resolve and by attuning to and trusting our guidance, but also by holding the hands of the others around us.

Quandary

I lived in NYC as a young adult. I remember seeing people who had no homes living on the street in the harsh winter. I rushed past them because I didn't have a solution. I didn't have the resources to help, and I was uncomfortable with them, with their plight. I was uncomfortable with those who were responsible for their situation and those who weren't. I was uncomfortable with making contact. Uncomfortable with my powerlessness. Uncomfortable with their vulnerability. I feared the ones who yelled out angrily, violently, having conversations with people who weren't there. I was scared of the suffering. I was afraid of a life in suspension, living moment to moment with seemingly no horizon to steer towards. A life without resources, dependent on finding food in garbage cans or the kindness of strangers.

But I have changed. Not my discomfort, and certainly, many situations are far too big for me to change as an individual. But I have more ability to help. I am not in the same position I was at that time. I can reach through the window into the immediate and less immediate world surrounding me and offer assistance when I choose, when it feels like the right thing to do.

When I do nothing, I feel I am ignoring the suffering. And I can get caught in a sense of powerlessness. But I am also not giving myself away as I did in the past. Now, I give while standing with a healthy respect for myself.

Connected to the world around me, I can engage with it rather than shut my heart and look away. And yet, I do not want to create dependency or a problem. If I feed all the deer, there will be fifty of them congregating, dependent on me. There is no quick or easy solution. Not with the deer, not with my illness. Not with the deep psychological issues that cause someone to misuse another.

I soften my dilemma by choosing to believe in reincarnation – even if I don't believe in linearity. I need a way to trust life, and I can only do so if I believe in a continuity of consciousness that extends beyond our bodies. If my life (or someone else's) is tragic, the learnings would transfer to the soul and not be lost, even as my body dissolved into dust. I can find no other way to reconcile what I wish for and see. I choose to trust.

I also choose to see through a lens of kindness. I choose to be kind in the moment. I choose to consider how my actions contribute to the future. I use my heart and consciousness to guide me.

Kindness

I remember when my awareness expanded to watching how I treated myself in each moment. I remember realizing the enormity of this awareness. With Alice, I was too kind to her, not kind enough to myself. Because I hadn't yet fully grown bones that could hold me. Because I could not honor my inner voice.

Because I had to descend again, I could shed and then rebuild.

In that descent, I found my no. I found my voice. That freed me up to choose how I would be kind rather than to compulsively acquiesce and see it as kindness, the compulsion being the engine, the kindness a deformed afterthought.

Sometimes, we have to protect ourselves or not get entangled in something not good for us. Other times, we can engage and help shift difficult situations. And always we have the choice to be kind. To open our hearts to ourselves. To see the part of ourselves that needs nurturing or care. To open our hearts to others. To share our positive perspectives and attitudes. To care about those who need us or are hungry. Even if we cannot get involved personally, our kind energy can help those who need it.

✶

After Loss

When I peer back
to the front of this life,
I see my small hand
folded warmly
into the large hand of my father.
My several steps matched his one
as if they were lined up to agree that way.
How could I love the same way today?

I remember towards the end,
my hands against his back,
pushing him up the too-steep hill
behind the house,
bones, bumpy through his thin shirt.
That is how I loved him at the end
in little bits and scraps,
where I was able.

I love you.
So hard, such a simple thing to say.
I stumbled through that wall
clumsily, knocked down that fear.
It was all I had to offer.
I could not explain to him
who he was to me.

I could not say
that I was being uprooted,
pulled up from the damp dark soil
of my childhood. I could not say
how my throat
kept swallowing at empty air
how my empty hands
hurt me.

Intense burning child
kicking fall leaves,
lost in moments passing.
What was time then?
I followed my father's footsteps
everywhere.

I look back
across the span of time
between then and now.
What was bright and shining
has softened. Fierce love
turned gentle, now
I love with care.

�֍

Increasing Light

My father died of pancreatic cancer in 1998, thirty-five days after he was diagnosed. I spent twenty of those days at our family home so I could be with him. I mostly sat with him as he slept, tried to get him what he needed, keep him comfortable. Sometimes, we talked a little. My father made peace with his life during this time. Said his life was as it should have been, that he had no regrets. And I could feel his love. His love for all of us. His love for his life. His acceptance of his dying.

As my father's body diminished, the light increased. I saw it gather inside of him. I saw it gather, increase, and become powerful. His body weaker, but the light bigger and bigger. That is a way of dying. As the body fades, the light intensifies.

I know I've increased light on this planet with the people I've worked with. In myself. I have done what I have been able to do and continue to do so. I do not know how to do more. We are living until we die. Until our next chapter, whatever that may be. We hold within our arms a basket of light, and like flower petals thrown before the bride, we scatter light everywhere. This is one of our powers. Like an incantation or magic spell, we brighten all that we touch.

May the light increase, spread, shower upon all of us as we move closer and closer to the end of our mother as we know her. As we learn to see beyond form to the beauty of the spirit within.

9
LOVE IS THE ROOT

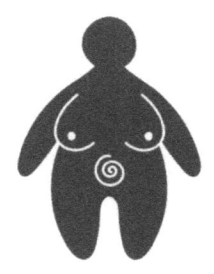

And now here is my secret, a very simple secret: It is only with the heart that one can see rightly; what is essential is invisible to the eye.
~ Antoine de Saint-Exupéry

※

Waterfall of Love

What is love, I ask you? The fairy tale? The happily ever after? No, that is not love. Love is a numinous pull so strong it may pull us under, into the dark, where we may run, or we may turn towards it and face the task of untangling what is tangled. Love at its best is transformative. Where two together do the work of maturing, transforming each other while tending the open wounds calling for healing.

What is there but love? The great rushing of the waterfall of love through the heart. Relational love has been a long, slow unraveling of bindings and knots for me. It has also been a gift beyond my imagination, for I did not see its fullness coming. Relational love requires a balance of you and me.

Without my husband and his support and love, many of my accomplishments would not have been able to fruit.

I was gifted this person, my husband, not only to learn to love but also to experience what the support of this kind of love feels like so I can lean back into it. And so, I could do the work and accomplish the mission that I came here to do.

I cannot imagine being on our earth without being nurtured or nurturing. Without soft touch or the tenderness of care. I think of being stung by a bee as a child and my mother tending to the welt. Without the warm hug of love, what an unforgiving, painful place it could be. It is harsh enough for many. I am one of the lucky ones. I found someone who I love and who loves me, and we have figured out how to heal our hurts and express our caring.

Support Enables

We live on this planet, our earth, which, despite its goodness, is where people abuse others, where burnings, stranglings, crucifixions, stonings, and so much more occur. How do we stand being here without love? I do not believe we can. So, I am kind to those I encounter. This hurt me in some ways when I was younger because I could not bear to disappoint anyone. I could not say no and could not take care of myself. I have learned to say no but also to stand in love. To know how important kindness is, to see how supporting someone enables them to go to much greater heights, to achieve things that would be impossible otherwise. I have seen what a lack of kindness does.

✯

LUMINOSITY

Light moves best

in a straight line.

It does not easily

navigate twists.

The twist must be straightened

The dark intention unbent.

The wicked self

transcended.

The polished gem will glow.

✹

Live Your Best Life

Because of this power of support, I gravitate to the spiritual world. It is why I love knowing that celestial beings walk beside us as we traverse through difficult times. It is why knowing that our challenges are temporary and part of our path while we are embodied is valuable. I see so many people stop their growth, get caught in fear, or damage others. What could they hold within that would help them to overcome their fear? An image? A thought? An affirmation? It doesn't matter what you pick. It doesn't matter if it is real. It matters that you find a way to live your best life.

What do witchy skills like channeling and hearing our inner voice matter if we don't come from our deep caring? A dark witch is a deformed witch. A witch with skill but a misshapen heart. The quality of our skill comes from the quality of our being. Imagine a luminous blue lapis gemstone bringing you a sense of peace – because that is one of the properties of lapis. We are each of us, gemstones, some deep fiery reds, others translucent lime, shocking transparent white or gentle amber, each with the potential to transmit something precious, distinct. Or we may be covered with dust, debris, and what comes through us does not offer enlightenment. We may be able to access information, but how useful is it if the debris we have not yet cleared away creates a warp in what we see or causes us to not care about the person we are engaged with, not see where they need help, where the welt of the bee sting needs soothing? Or if we don't use the information we receive wisely – to better someone or something?

I think of a woman raised to believe she is not good enough.

This false self-understanding will stop her from reaching for her heart's desire. It may prevent her from seeing where another person needs to reach to find their heart's desire. It limits her vision, changes her positive influence. I think of my ex-husband. The shame he experienced growing up limited him. He pushed it away. Rather than experience shame, he gravitated towards anger. A more powerful feeling. Our anger can be useful. It can also be a poison. And skilled or not, we can poison ourselves with our attitudes and actions. What we transmit is then tainted.

Learning to love is the slow peeling away of all that is not love. It is the releasing of the trauma, the pain, the shame. It is allowing feelings to fully flow, evolve, and grow, opening to a tender caring and recognition that we all struggle, we all feel, we all deserve.

※

Seagull Spirit

The water sparkles.

A gull is overhead,

screaming, squawking.

Huge wings reach wide, flap,

cut through the air.

The gull looks, sees.

I see, I see, I see.

I see from above.

The perspective changes.

The angle shifts.

My instincts lead.

I see see see.

My Sense of Home

It is December of 2014, and three weeks since my much-loved husband almost died. Although he is here now, when I imagine my life without him, I realize there is no place to go, nothing to do that could feel okay. I feel homeless, lost, and adrift.

What is home but a tender heart we connect with? What is home other than acceptance and love? How two different beings hold hands, the pink of the tourmaline harmonizes or shocks against the emerald. Our uniqueness seen and honored in the jewel of the heart. Our aloneness softened.

What I would like in this ever-changing world is for my connection to god to be my home. I would like my ballast to be a conscious connection with the divine, with unwavering truth, peace, safety, and love. Instead, events shake me, leave me undulating like the waves outside our house, shimmering light and shadow – one moment bright, the next dim, lost.

Near Death

Mike is writhing and unable to sleep from a sharp stabbing pain in his ribs. It is the night before his hernia surgery. We are in a hotel near the hospital. The pain is so powerful he cannot fully lie down, and we tie a bathrobe belt tight, clenched around his chest, creating pressure to help contain the intensity. My small inner voice saying wait, something is wrong. Something is wrong. But I am not able to convince him to delay the surgery he has waited months for. The mechanism of the hospital schedules of the surgeon and his assembly line of surgeries had no room for my knowing.

This event of my husband's near-death could not have unfolded any other way. Mike is strong and, at times, stubborn. Like Zeus, he is more connected to his invincibility than his mortality and vulnerability. He believes he is right even when he isn't (don't we all?). A closed mind is sometimes opened in increments event by event. Sometimes, the pain must reach a certain intensity before a person will listen, not unlike the Leonard Cohen quote, "There is a crack in everything; that's how the light gets in."

After the surgery, he was sick, even sicker than before. Shaking, chills, coughing and knife-cutting pain. He increased his pain meds. We tried CBD. He seemed slightly better, but only for a short time. Neither of us knew how sick he really was. As each opportunity to get help came and passed, and he became sicker and sicker, I became more and more agitated. I didn't know why. I just didn't feel right. And getting medical help where we live is not quick or easy. We live on an island. There is not a hospital here. Medical resources are limited.

In the car driving to a doctor on the island a few days later, Mike is shaking uncontrollably. I cover him with a blanket to help him feel warmer and to try to stop his shaking. His body is having trouble regulating his temperature. Something is terribly wrong. Does he have pleurisy, a pulled muscle, costochondritis? The doctor suggests tests on the mainland. But Mike wants to get comfortable, not go for more tests. The idea of a trip in his condition seems beyond comprehension. He takes Percocet around the clock, cough medicine, and a small pharmacy of other items. I pull hope to me. Hold onto it. Try to believe the delusion that he might be improving.

He gets worse. The coughing increases, and the pain. He goes to see his primary care nurse practitioner. She takes a blood test, diagnoses pneumonia, and gives him antibiotics. But the pain continued to increase, and the cold sweats and shaking got worse. The coughing. The blood in the coughing. Mike does not tell me. I do not know.

Gap

The gap left in a life when the body exits is overwhelming. The sense of loss and loneliness – the desire to find a way to touch what was. Across the boundaries between here and there are those I have loved who have passed. My cat Hank, my father, mother, grandparents. My baby pony Nichol with his rotund body and soft gray fur, my horse Specks, and countless others who once peopled my world and gifted me with their presences. With some of those passings, my sense of home crashed and broke. And what of them? Without form, are they still bashed about, as I sometimes feel? Do they still feel pain, loss, abandonment, grief? Are they happy? No longer in this world, do they feel a sense of home?

Increasing Pressure

Mike's body is failing. But his will is formidable. There is no way to maneuver around it. Then, three weeks or so into this misidentified and still unidentified illness, Mike's left leg swelled up huge. He shows it to me the next day. I am terrified. Another piece of a glacier falls into the sea. Another piece of wrong, wrong, wrong becoming visible. Earlier that day, I had talked to Nicole, the healer I work with.

She says something is wrong. Red flag. His circulation isn't right. His organs are stressed. Something black in his lungs. My sense of internal pressure increases.

Delay

At my insistence, Mike goes to see the nurse practitioner again to check on his leg. She takes blood to test and see if he has a clot. It is a Friday. The results could come back later that day, or Saturday or Monday. She suggests he get more tests on the mainland in a day or two or after the weekend. I am shrieking inside. Barely able to contain myself. A few days? Is everyone crazy? I race to the computer and Google blood clots. It was now obvious why his leg swelled. Blood clots are life-threatening. Get help immediately, the articles said. Mike wanted to wait for the test results. Perhaps they would be back that day. The idea of the ferry ride when sick was daunting.

Then, it is evening, and the ferries are finished for the day. The test results had not come in. I am frantic. I push harder. I force my will against his. I become stronger. I will not stop. Mike agrees to go to the emergency room the next day, on Saturday, rather than wait till Monday as he wished to do.

Another Voice

That night, I am looking at Mike sitting in the living room chair he will sleep in because he cannot comfortably lie down. My body is screaming. I cannot get it to stop. I cannot make myself quiet down. I will not sleep. I know he will be dead in the morning. It is that simple.

I see his death approaching, see it shadowed around him. It will happen by morning. I don't know what to do. I call a woman who dog sits for us to see if she is available for the next day. I tell her what is happening. Tell her what I know. She insists I call the fire department right away.

Her voice backs up mine. It is all I need, that piece of support. I tell Mike I am calling the fire department. He does not have a choice at this point. But he says okay. I call. Then I call 911.

Thank You

In five minutes, we have three people in our home. In ten minutes more, we have a houseful of EMTs and paramedics. (Thank you!) They put him on oxygen and a gurney. Off we go in the ambulance to the airport. Then, onto the plane and to the hospital in Anacortes. I begin to feel relieved. We spend the night there having tests done. I see the ugly dark black running through the ultrasound image. His entire left leg, from knee to groin, is clotted. Three lobes of his lungs are filled with clots. The doctor says this is too dangerous and too much for the medical capabilities of their hospital. She starts looking for a more equipped hospital to send him to. She is worried that at any moment, another clot could shut down his lungs entirely and kill him.

I lay on the hard cement floor of his hospital room. It is the middle of the night; I wait for them to find him a hospital with a bed. He isn't safe yet. Another clot could dislodge from his leg and move into his lungs. I pray. *Please be okay. Please give us enough time. Please find him a bed.* Finally, at five in the morning, we are ambulanced to Seattle.

A few hours later, two ICV filters are placed in his veins to stop more clots from migrating to his lungs. He is given a new drug to prevent future clots. The doctor tells him he is extremely fortunate. He should have died the first few hours after the clotting started. He should have died three weeks ago. Finally, he is safe but so fragile, like a thin, hurt bird.

Hindsight

Mike had been dying in front of me for three weeks. I didn't know it consciously, but part of me did. Inside, I could barely stand it. I had felt trapped. I had felt as if a suffocating weight was lying on top of me and pinning me down. Inside, a part of me was shrieking.

I couldn't escape the feeling. I couldn't get the blocks to open and make things happen. Until everything followed its logical course, and eventually, the path to help did open – albeit in a dramatic and dangerous way. I now see the synchronicities that allowed this: the process over the weeks leading to a release into assistance and an opening into Mike's acceptance of his humanness and mortality and my acceptance of using my entire will to initiate correct action.

Time

I look at the eons of time that precede and follow our togetherness. This short span (over six years together when this occurred) is nothing when I think of the time it takes for carbon to become a diamond or a universe to unfold and expand.

Our short human lives so precious and so fleeting, and yet I have moments with my husband that feel eternal. Moments subtle but also so significant, that I lean into them with all of myself. I feel wrapped in friendship and caring. Those moments are finite. I will lose them someday – no matter who dies first. How do I hold onto them when I cannot? How do I tuck these moments into my heart so that perhaps they can nourish me when we are both long gone and dust? So they can stay with me even as I am in another time and space, another reality, another life.

Old Friends

I look back now and see my battle – the fight against my inner knowing. The old criticisms now internalized that stopped me from claiming my feelings, my knowing. *Why do you always feel so much? Why do you cry? Why do you get upset so easily?* I remember the childhood accusations that were harsher than those words. "Cry baby." "She's so emotional, so dramatic." "Drama Queen." Those old parts of me – those shamed parts are my friends. My body that feels and knows what the mind may not recognize. So many of us have put away this part of ourselves to our detriment. It wasn't until my knowing was affirmed by our dog sitter that I was able to move into action. The universe, finding the best way to mobilize help, guided me to call her.

My husband did not see his death approaching. He does not have my sensitivity. That is my gift, not his. It is my gift that was instrumental in saving his life.

Truth Sayer

Obedience – the practice or virtue of submission to a higher power or authority. When did submission become a virtue? A noisy screaming self is sometimes precisely what is needed. Is this over? Of course not. Mike may not want to honor his fragility. He has a substantial will and wants to do what he wants. But I will not push away my discomfort and intuition again. I will fight harder. Scream louder. I want him to live more than I want him to feel as if everything is okay, as if he is in charge or in control, an illusion at best. I can speak the truth now; say the words I couldn't say before.

Temporary Eclipse

I have built my sense of home slowly. I remember years ago, alternating between regular life and days of intense darkness, having descended into an altered reality, a loss of perspective, depression. I knew then that I had fallen and learned how to crawl myself out. It wasn't quick or easy, but I could do it. I could remember there was light on the other side, that this wasn't the only reality. I learned the eclipse was temporary. I began to build a sense of home – not home with another, so much as home within myself.

In my previous not-so-great marriage, I found a sense of home in developing a stronger relationship with myself. I found it in the path of my career – the people I spent time with and the work I did. I had a bigger outer world because I needed nourishment outside of that relationship.

And although that divorce was traumatic, I still had parts of my life that filled that need for home.

Impermanence

I get caught. Like the fly in the spider web, I struggle, try to rip myself out of my dilemma. Do I find god in detaching from what is impermanent, or do I find god in appreciating the beauty of what is impermanent? I pick the latter. The feminine face of god, the embodied. I watch with delight the gray-feathered blue heron lurching across the wet winter yard. I delight in the temporal, the trees shifting in the wind, their tall, solid bodies reaching upward. I delight in the burst of pink of the apple blossom and the swooping of the swallows that nest under the eaves.

I feel grief as our world changes, as diversity collapses, as other beings, even entire species, die.

That is the piece I struggle with. Death and transformation. If I could hold on tight and keep everything dear close to me – I would. It would be a more static and predictable world. I know that isn't the answer.

Where are all those beings who have peopled my world with love now that they are no longer physically here? How do I reach them? How do I nourish myself when I have been left to live without the cloak of their love?

Temporal Gift

Outside, it is windy, darkening, gray blue water, silvers, and mauves. Mike is slowly getting better. Our home is cozy and warm. We have a fire in the fireplace. I am grateful we both are here, grateful for this time we have together. The gift of the temporal is a more acute awareness of the specialness of this time, of each moment. I am left with gratitude for my relationship, my life; gratitude for the eternity of each moment, even as I know it will end.

I don't know how we survive these losses. I don't know how to hold on without holding on. I don't know how to trust this thing we call god when, for me, home, and god is holding my kitty Hank or my dog Nutmeg, sitting on the body of this green planet, being with my husband.

✺

Sacred

- to make holy - whole

The dew drop clinging to the branch.
A world reflected inside.
Perfect, clear, bright, glistening.

I open my eyes and see what is already there.
See through the eyes of Da'at - the center.
The seeing makes it holy.

The gift of positive sight.
The link of the sight and the heart.
Yes, I see you. Yes, you are sacred.

Intimacy

"Will you cuddle me?" my husband asked. "No, I'm reading," I say, a bit put out that he cannot see I am otherwise occupied. *Christ, I sound like my mother,* I think to myself. My mother who I do not want to be like. My mother who was cut off from her feelings. My mother, who loved me but did not know how to show it, who could not reach out and bridge the gap between us. My mother, who I felt unloved and unseen by.

Mother Wound

In 2012, my husband and I visited my mother at her home on Oak Island, North Carolina. I had been sick for a few years with undiagnosed Lyme Disease. I was exhausted, and the cross-country trip to visit her was a stretch. But it was an attempt to reach out to her, to build on the connection I felt with her when Mike and I married earlier that year.

My mother lives alone. My father had died years before. This is her summer cottage, where she escapes from the cold Pennsylvania winters. My husband has never been here before. I haven't been here in more than fifteen years.

My husband and I are in her house, sitting on the old plaid couch in the dusty living room, waiting for her. Her home is filled with things. And not clean. I am uncomfortable waiting in her house because I am concerned about my health.

She lives close to the beach, walking distance. It is beautiful there, especially off-season as it is now when there are few people, more birds, gulls, sandpipers, shells.

"Mom, let's go for a short walk to the beach."
"In a little while, honey, I'm busy," she called out from her bedroom.
"Do you need any help?" I holler.
"No," she responds.

We wait. And wait. I page through some magazines. I walk around my mother's living room and look at the bits of her life there. Pottery she has made. Paintings of my father's. Shells and sea glass from the beach.

Relaxed at first, my feelings begin to intensify. Over an hour later, I blow up.

"We are going to leave," I scream, crying. Mom comes into the room, alarmed, perplexed. I continue, "We came all the way here to see you, and you aren't even going to spend time with us? What are you doing that is so important it can't wait?" I am confused, tired, upset, and angry. My heart hurts. I feel like a kid again. Invisible. Unappreciated. How did I regress so quickly?

"I was trying to hook up Magic Jack. I need to get it taken care of," she explained. (Magic Jack was my mother's way of getting free telephone service through her computer.) "Why are you so upset?"

I couldn't describe to her how she was. How she missed every cue for connection. How she got caught in being right, with a touch of indignation.

 I could only blather on about how I came all that way to see her, and it seemed as if she had no interest in being with me.

Innocent

My mother was innocent. She did not see how her behavior hurt me. She was merely following the dictates of habit and her nature. Not easily able to see another perspective, she lived within the confines of her own needs.

This story between us is an old one. It goes back to the beginning of our relationship. It goes back to her willfulness and my sensitivity and fear. It goes back to her pushing me in the swimming pool when I am three or four years old at my first swimming lesson.

I am afraid of the water and hesitant to get in. She pushes me in from behind, a surprise attack when I am not looking. Our story goes back to her carrying me in the ocean as a young child, I am clinging to her, afraid of the big water, and she drops me in, hoping I will overcome my fear instead of understanding how I retract when I am frightened, how I will move out slowly when I feel safe. She pushed instead of providing comfort. She did not want such a dependent child.

Similarly, I am innocent. So is my husband. When he asked to cuddle, he just wanted to connect with me while I was happy to be in my separate space for a bit before trying to sleep. I put my book down and turn over, pull myself against him. He is warm, and soon, his breathing evens out. He is asleep.

I am grateful for him in my life. I am thankful for his love, for his connection. I am grateful for his support and companionship. I want him to know that. To feel it. And he usually does. My gratitude allows for more intimacy in my marriage.

Silver Strand

There is a delicate line between each of us in a relationship. A thin silver strand that links us, connects us, and yet lets us know we are separate. We can pay attention to this connection or reside in our more insular reality. We can forget the fragility of what is between us, the need to feel loved and precious.

My husband doesn't know, didn't feel pushed away when I wanted to read. He accepted my separate space and was willing to wait. It was I who was impacted more strongly. For me, it was a moment of clarity.

Because of the family I grew up in, because of how we were not valued, one of my triggers is not being seen, not being listened to. Not being noticed. I can take things personally because it seems he doesn't care or doesn't see me as I am in a particular moment.

But he does care. He cares a lot, and his care nourishes me. I want to remember that his needs do not mean I am not seen or loved. We are simply two different continents, and in each moment, we can close the door between us or open it.

Gathered

I am aware. I have the capacity for self-reflection, insight, and a new response. My awareness is like a fine living net that reaches over and gathers the different parts of myself together. It allows me to see what is. It allows me to watch myself. It isn't that awareness stops me from my immediate response, but that with it, I can see myself: how I responded, what I missed, what I want to change. My awareness is a gift.

We are more than our habits, reactions, and defenses – how we are wired. Yet, we live within our wiring, within our structure.

With awareness, I can slowly unwind the strands of myself that dictate how I react, where I get activated. I can evolve to attain who I wish to be instead of staying stuck in old habits that developed as I was growing up. I can change to allow the better parts of me to come forward, to take the front stage, and run the show.

My disconnections are much more subtle than my mother's. I do not have the same difficulty with emotions that she had.

I have spent years in therapy, years becoming a therapist, and years studying human connection, support, and communication. I have learned how to be myself in a way that allows truer relating. I have spent a lifetime correcting the deficits of my past, climbing out of the deep pit of my wounds.

In my earlier life, I had to learn human basics that others grow up with, like hugging and saying, "I love you." These simple acts of support and contact were not part of the family I grew up in.

They did not come naturally to me. Initially, they felt foreign and uncomfortable, shameful to be so vulnerable.

Balance

Despite the subtlety of the interaction between myself and my husband, I can feel the part of me that takes it personally that my space and separate needs aren't being respected. How my wiring automatically pulled me into that perception instead of another one, like "How sweet of him."

Love is a living, breathing thing. It occurs from moment to moment within and between us. At any second, we can look at ourselves and change our course. We can find the balance between me and we. This is the power we have. The power to express. The power to change. The power to be the love we wish to receive.

Today

Would have been the eighty-sixth birthday of my mother.
I sit with a friend, and we pull tarot cards.
We pull cards for my mother.

Three.

The Lovers.
Judgment.
Two of Cups.

All upright.

I have been emotional today.
I feel my mother's presence. A light breeze.

She has visited me over the last seven years.
Playing with the pendulum, it sometimes behaves in a nonsensical way.
I know someone is visiting.
I ask who.
Sometimes Hank. Sometimes my mother.

The Lovers - I know she loves me.
She tells me.
Judgment - Awakening. Rebirth.

There is no longer a block between us.
She is in a good place.
She is clear to give.
I am clear to receive.
Two of Cups - Happiness, relationships, love.

A healing has settled.
We are restored.
My mother has not wandered off in this other dimension.

She pays attention.
She visits with love.
She has looked at herself,
situated herself.
She comes through.
She is present.
The skin of her limitations gone.
Her energy light, warm, bright.

Thank you.

My Mother's Passing

My mother died July 22, 2014, after a yearlong battle fighting a rare and deadly cancer, mucosal melanoma. It was the day before my birthday, and I wasn't there. Perhaps she picked that day to spare me her death occurring on my birthday. We had thought she would last longer. I had a visit planned.

My brother, sister, and aunt were with her as she took her last breaths and released herself from her diminished body. My grief at not being there was enormous. My awareness of my own failings, clear.

Stuck

I had last seen my mother just over two months earlier for Mother's Day. I was there to honor her, cook for her, clean her home. I was there because I didn't think she would be around for another Mother's Day, and I wanted her to feel loved.

During that visit, we had a big blowout – or, more correctly, I had one. I was trying to open the pantry cupboard in my mother's kitchen to make her a meal. These cupboards, which have been part of my life for at least forty-five years, have heavy giant doors with little, tiny rollers. They fall off the rollers and jam constantly. I was in the middle of cooking when the doors jammed and wouldn't move. I pushed and pulled. I swore and complained. My aunt came in to help me. They wouldn't budge. I felt it was a metaphor – you may want to connect with me, but I am not accessible. That was the message I heard, and it was as if my mother's very house was speaking for her.

Forty-five years of frustration emerged as my aunt and I tried to get the cupboard doors opened. Mom, resting in the next room, heard us and came into the kitchen to see what the fuss was about. She was angry with me for messing up the doors, blamed me. But underneath, I think she was frustrated with herself, with her body and disease. She was frustrated that I was upset and things were not going smoothly.

She tried to move those heavy, stuck doors herself with her frail, weak, and dying body. Something snapped in me.

The Wall

I screamed, "I hate this." Meaning, I hate that I cannot reach you, meaning I hate that I cannot help you because you have never dealt with your difficulty with emotion, all of the blocks between us. I threw a broken vase (another item of the multitude of useless things piled about and filling every square inch of space, another piece of the "stuff" between us) into the yard.

Mom began to lecture me about being emotional. "There is no reason to get upset. Stop it. Stop being upset," – but underneath, I could feel her fear of my feelings and intensity.

"I'm upset for a reason," I said. "I'm not attacking you. I am trying to help you." Couldn't she see that? Why was she yelling at me? I said, "I am your daughter. I love you. I'm trying to help you, and I can't. Why are you so angry at me when I am trying to help you?"

Then I told her that she sounded like her mother. Her mother who pushed everyone away with her sharp tongue.
"What did you do about your mother?" I asked.
"I left," she said.
"Do you want me to leave?" I asked.
"No," she said.

She looked right at me then. She said, "I can't change. My feelings are locked away. I'm all walled off. I can't find that part of myself. I can't do it."

I stopped. There was nowhere to go. She saw the block inside her.

She knew what I was talking about. She couldn't do it and told me so directly. The air went out of me. It was a very real moment and the end of our conversation. I couldn't make her connect. I had to accept her limitations.

Separate Spaces

I didn't reach out and hug her. It didn't even occur to me. We went back into our separate spaces. A brief opening of honesty, and then the space between us closed. Here we were, two people who loved each other, who couldn't reach for each other. She couldn't show me her need for connection. I couldn't make her be able to connect with me. I didn't know how to reach past her wall and touch her. What could be sadder than that?

It wasn't either of our faults. We had such different ways of being in our lives. I feel connected by sharing insights, understandings, what I am learning or perceiving.

She felt connected by chatting about the weather, what the relatives were up to, and how many thistles she had pulled up that day. I needed her to be more emotional and to accept my emotions. She simply wasn't good at emoting and nurturing. She was trapped in her own limitations. I had pulled back years before as I had given up on connecting with her long ago.

I realized how much I didn't know how to reach her; how hard she was for me to understand and accept fully. In short, I saw where I had failed her and where we had failed each other.

Pink Lady Slippers

At our memorial service for her, her friends talked about her as a woman I knew only peripherally.

They spoke of how she would call them and invite them for a walk deep into the woods to see the pink lady slippers blooming. They spoke of the loveliness of her spirit. They talked about their connection with her. They talked about a real woman with whom they had a real relationship. Somehow, without our family history, these relationships were easier for her. She was accepted and loved for who she was, and she was able to love back. These friends saw the part of her that was beautiful.

Now that she is gone, I see not only how much I couldn't be there for her but also how much I needed her. I can see how she wasn't able to transcend her own limitations, and neither was I. My intensity may have reminded her of her mother's. Blocked her ability to truly see me. Her rejection of this part of me, my big feeling self, wounded me.

Whispers

I sometimes feel my mother's spirit; I feel her presence around me. Her energy feels happy. I have a sense of her beauty. She whispers that she feels young again without her body. She tells me that she loves me, that she is sorry she didn't know how to connect with me while she was on the planet. I feel closer to her now than when she was in body. I talk to her in a way we never talked when she was alive. "I wish we could have done it differently," I say. "I wish I had known how to understand and accept you. I wish we could have been closer. I wish I had found a way to bridge the gap between us." I know that she wishes she, too, had more capacity to love, that she hadn't walled herself off so strongly from her feelings.

I know my mother loved me, loves me, and I loved her too, deep down.

I know she wishes she had done better, just as I wish I had done better in our relationship. I can feel her love now in a way I could not before. Since her death, our relationship has changed.

I think back to who she was, and I feel empathy for her – for all of us and this incredibly challenging process of living. I look back and see how large and scary she was for me at one time – and how integral and essential.

My mother needed me to love and accept her. She needed me to see beneath her emotionally constricted self. She needed me to accept that when I told her that I loved her, and she said, "Okay," that meant she loved me back; that was her way of saying, "I love you too." My father was able to joke with her and make her feel cared for.

My need for her to be different and my disappointments that had accumulated over the years were too large.

Imprint

In a drawer, I have an old iPhone. It has a voicemail my mother left me shortly before her death. I have not listened to the recording. Nor have I gotten rid of the phone. I cannot seem to throw away this imprint of her, her last message to me. She is gone, or at least not here in the physical anymore. But this ghost of hers, this vibration, this message, is still here.

For me, her voice, what she is saying, is different than a picture of her. Really, it isn't, but it feels different to me.

And so, I keep the phone in a drawer – a stalemate of some kind. I know it is there. I do not listen to it. I cannot bear to hear her voice. I cannot bear to throw it away. Perhaps someday I will be able to listen to her voice, trembly. Perhaps, someday, I will be able to let that part of her go.

Bridging

I no longer blame her. What is in our hearts does not always come through our bodies. We each have our own limited vistas. We are each doing our best. Sometimes, the gap is big, and we do not know how to bridge it. Sometimes, the love that is there is not able to emerge and be expressed. Sometimes, our hurt is too great for us to risk being vulnerable.

Mom, please forgive me for pulling away from you. Please forgive me for not being able to accept you fully. Please forgive me for wanting more than you could give. Please forgive me for not seeing the beauty of your soul. I am so sorry. I am sorry I could not find a bigger part of myself with you. I am so sorry for the parts of me that were not love.

I miss so much what we never had. I miss the relationship that wasn't. And yet, I feel a sense of gratitude for her giving me this deep look at myself. Thank you for what you did give to me. Thank you for being with me now. I am grateful for your presence and our new relationship.

I love you.

✻

TRANSITION

I am leaving. My body shrinking.
Onward to somewhere else. My time here is ending.
Complete for now.

I leave behind a life lived the best I knew how.
I release regret. I release all.

I claim what was.
Yes, I loved you.
Yes, I loved me.

My spirit enlivens. My heart opens.

I am love, and love wants to flow.
The future awaits. Freedom from form.

✹

Last Moments

I found a photograph of my father and myself the other day. I am thirty-seven years old. He is sixty-seven. It was taken a year before he died. He looks happy, his arm across my shoulder and mine gingerly around his waist. Some families don't touch. Ours did not. I am smiling awkwardly. He looks more comfortable. I wish I had held on tighter, that I hadn't felt so awkward. I could see it in the photo, only half a hug given for the camera. How could I have known, so little time? How could I push through that awkwardness into feeling good, glad, comfortable with that uncomfortable touch?

In 1998, my father began and finished dying. I was with him for much of it. While my father was dying, his body whitening, withering on the bed where he spent most of his final days, I would sit with him. Sometimes I would talk. Mostly, though, I would just be with him.

I look at a thin scrap of paper, the picture of us, remembering. My body trembles. Shock. I am flooded with the thought of him lying in my parents' bedroom. He is under a white sheet. I sit beside him, read. Sometimes, I hold his hand. He wakes up, disoriented, surprised. Happy to see me. Outside, it is a brilliant green, beautiful. Bright. Leaves like stained glass filter emerald light into their bedroom.

Inside dim, quiet except for the wheezing of the machine to keep his mattress moving in little ups and downs, like breathing, a slow in and out, so his skin wouldn't sit too long in one spot and develop weeping sores.

Ready

It will be my thirty-eighth birthday in a day or so. Dad will try to sing to me, Happy Birthday, wobbly, trembling, barely able to sit up. I will cry. It will be a day filled with pain. The catheter won't go in; it will stab. I will rub his back, as will the nurse, feel his long, thin bones, help him sit until the muscles relax, the pain subsides. He will be asking how much longer, how much longer until he gets to die.

Later still, several days, after enough morphine to kill three men or a horse when he is gasping deep unconscious breaths, his mouth open, his chest rattling up and down, I will take his hand. I stare down at it. There is nothing there. His hand feels empty of life, limp, heavy. Vacant. Slowly, I rub my thumb back and forth across thin, papery skin, across the hand I haven't touched since childhood. I hold his heavy hand in mine just in case he is somehow still there.

Lightened

He changed a lot in those final days. He lightened. He accepted. He released the torment he carried. He became at peace. I could see the spirit grow stronger as his body became less and less, waning, falling in on itself. I wonder about this loss, this dying of a body I love, of the bodies I have loved, if, at the same time, there is a lightening, a releasing, a reaching, and a blossoming?

The bright light that blooms as death draws nearer.

Strengths

I learn from this loss, from this exit of the physical. I learn as I watch my father die and see spirit expand as form melts away. I learn as my heart aches for a man both cruel and brilliant. I learn as he says, "I don't regret a moment of my life." As he embraces all that he was, the good and the bad. The ugly and the beautiful. A different strength than mine. Mine is the strength to excavate, dig into pain, reorganize, release. Transform. Something he did not do. His is the strength to own himself completely, to release all doubt, to stand in himself. I can learn from this. I do.

Gift of Love

Our time in this life is scarce in the vastness of all that is and teaches us to love what is here right now, for it shall not always be. I pull that challenge to myself. I claim it. I mold myself around it. I allow it to guide me, feed me, nourish me. Appreciation is born of love and impermanence.

Like the snowflake falling, delicate white crystal high in the air, gravity pulling, it may stay for a while or melt as it lands, every moment, every relationship, every life unique and fleeting.

Learning to love is one of the challenges of an imperfect world, imperfect others, imperfect self. Relationships can be difficult. They can hurt. Shape us. Challenge us. We may close our hearts, distance ourselves, carry wounds for decades. Yet underneath, there is a potential to love, whether love of self or love of others. Whether it is the love of learning what these challenges bring or a love of the kaleidoscope of moments we travel through, the ever-changing terrain.

We learn through states of being. Ice becomes water, becomes steam, becomes water again. Oh, I am this and this and this. Oh, I will not always be this. I will not always be here. You will not always be here.

Loving gifts us with the opportunity to transform. To become more than we were. To bridge gaps, to mend, to feel gratitude and appreciation. Real love takes us out of our insular selves. Our lives become offerings, caldrons where alchemy takes place, where lead becomes gold, where opposites can find union. Where the divinity of ourselves can shine. This is another step in our individuation, our self-actualization. This is another step in claiming our power to breathe out with love, transforming and enlivening all we touch. And it is in love that we find our true home.

❈

10
Our Living Journey

I shall always remember how the peacocks' tails shimmered when the moon rose amongst the tall trees, and on the shady bank the emerging mermaids gleamed fresh and silvery amongst the rocks...
~ Hermann Hesse

Expect a Miracle

2010. I drive, wind along the road, watch the houses, trees, fields, more houses, exit the town, more space, higher, twisting road, through canyons and mountains. Hope, hope, hope. I drive for nearly an hour. To a small, remote, and rural community on the top of a hill. To a witch, a shaman, a healer.

Dr. Russel. In his white coat. His hair, eyes, wild. He runs a small clinic. His intuition and scientific knowledge are both considerable.

Please help me.
I am seeing him because I am very sick. My Lyme disease still five years from being diagnosed.

I lay down on his massage table. The white paper covering his table crunches. I feel vulnerable. Eyes upward. I see, taped to the ceiling, a little piece of paper, "Expect a Miracle." Oh. A new thought.

That little note opened me up. I hadn't been thinking about miracles. I had been thinking about how much I was suffering and how powerless and confused I felt. I had felt trapped, not expansive.

Opened Mind
That message has flashed through my mind a hundred times over the last ten years. Every time I think of it, I remember that our trajectories can change. What is, is not what will always be.

Conditions are not static. We engage, interact, influence, bring into being. We add thought, prayer, emotion, hope to the mix. The world evolves, and we with it. The universe expands, the planets move. Galaxies are born and die. The dust is swept up by the wind, swirls, resettles, a new pattern.

Life is not dead. Still. Stopped.

That message opened me up to the possibility that things would change. To the possibility of the extraordinary and amazing. To an open mind.

Expect a miracle. It filled me with hope. It made me remember the world I live in, that I am not inconsequential. It gave me hope that when we are stuck or suffering, it will not be forever. Hope that the universe is big and miracles do happen.

I carry that message around inside me now. And sometimes, it pops into my head just when I need it.

Expect

Once, a long time ago
a woman said to me
imagine you are sending out
invitations. What
will the universe send back?

Sometimes
a window is opened
so crisp air
and sun sparks
can enter.

Remember
the sun
in all its glory
lighting
bud and leaf.

The snore
of a beloved dog
eyes closed, released.

That
there will be another day,
an easier one.

This one
just a moment in
the passing of time
possibilities pushing
the lid open.

Magic Means Miracle

Magic means miracle. It means there is more than we know. It means something can happen that we never dreamed. Magic is the soft gray rain splashing on the deck, moistening the world. Magic is meeting someone who changes your life. Magic is possibility, beauty, and freedom. Magic is the feeling of delight.

Magic has always been important to me. It could be the magic of nature, like a patch of bright green moss on the north side of a rock with its soft undulating texture, or the magic of the mist rolling up Topanga Canyon Boulevard in the mountains near Los Angeles. It could be the magic of a dream that imparted information to me. It could be the chill that runs down my body when I experience a knowing or recognize a truth. There are so many kinds of magic and magical experiences.

When I look back at my life, I can see my path unfold with purpose, a pattern that has emerged. For me, this, too, is magic, the magic of creating my life, the magic of walking through and participating in the unfolding of time. The magic of knowing the universe is good.

Immanence

My friend, Shelly, once shared an experience she had with me. She was eating a bowl of barley and had an enlightened moment where she could feel god within the grain. This wasn't a thought. It was a full-body experience of joy, love, and union with god. An experience like this cannot be easily put into words. In this case, words are an empty shell that merely explain an understanding of what occurred. It is only through the lyricism and dance of poetry that words come close to making the experience alive.

I imagine the grain of barley glowing, pulsing, alive. I imagine my friend's entire body lit up as she chewed and swallowed the kernel. I imagine her in a kaleidoscope of vibrating colors, radiating out, connecting with every molecule of the universe, her full self blooming open and alive.

For me, the idea of living in a magical universe, where possibilities we cannot imagine exist, is expansive and nourishing.

Transcendence

Magic is connected to transcendence. Transcendent means we rise above; we are beyond the scope of ordinary experience. When I have the feeling of awe, I am in a transcendent state. Often, we find transcendent experiences through psychotropic drugs. When I took DMT and mushrooms, the experiences I had were transcendent, experiences that helped me know there was more to my life than what I usually lived, how I usually perceived. Sometimes, a knowing arrives, and, in that moment, a sense of connection to the universe or god is experienced. These moments are not fully describable. Yet they are part of our lived experience.

Humanity has lived under the weight of the banal and the pressures of subsistence for eons. So much of our lives involves routines ensuring survival. We may be worn down as we struggle to eat, struggle to stay alive and not be killed, struggle not to be enslaved, struggle to endure.

We long to leave suffering behind and find a re-member-ing of who we really are. We desire transcendence. We long to rise above mundane reality to a world filled with magic and possibility. Magic is a counterpoint to struggle.

Magic is the purple crocus lifted up out of the snow to share its brilliance. Magic is the place where more possibilities exist, and miracles present themselves.

I live in ordinary reality, a reality where I get sick, where I struggle, where I have doubts and fears. A reality where I have work to do whether I feel like it or not, but there is another part of me that stretches beyond that reality. There is a part of me that lives in magic, possibility, and transcendence. There is a part of me that breathes in nature and breathes out poetry. That part needs to be acknowledged and honored. That part needs more than food, shelter, air, and water. That part needs imagination, art, poetry, myth, magic, and god. That part of me has embraced magic and healing work.

Aligning

Affirmation, prayer, and healing work are techniques of magic used to bring about positive change in the physical world by working with will, energy, and alignment. We send healing energy to others and know that it may calm them, soothe them, help them – even if they cannot hear what we have to say. Sometimes, I sit down and get quiet. I send energy to a person or situation. I ask that they feel support or that a situation be resolved. Sometimes, I feel a shift occur.

A magical world-view opens our vision, stretches our horizons, sees possibility rather than limitation. When we have a magical

worldview, we do not diminish persistence, patience, or hard work to reach our goals, but we expand beyond them to allow for possibilities not imagined. We set intentions because we know the universe is alive.

We know that if we align ourselves with harmonious or wise energies, we are allowing them to influence our lives for the better. This is different than magical thinking, where we believe what we want will just happen. Magic involves open expectation and delight, the application of vision, energy, and intent, not delusion.

This brings up the idea of faith in the universe. Faith in the universe is not a static picture. Not the little person staring up into the sky and seeing god as a parent who will take care of everything. I offer a different idea. I received an image the other day. I was asking my guides about abundance. "Help me understand abundance," I asked. I saw a funnel that opened both upward and downward in my mind. It opened up to the universe, and universal energy flowed through it. I was the narrow part of the funnel, the conduit. The universal energy flowed through me, the channel, and through my actions, the energy moved out into our planet, assisting those I focused on or had contact with. I saw clearly how we co-create, how we are conduits. How we can be part of the good of the universe. Who we are and what we do has everything to do with the magic that manifests.

Living Web

I see the magic of the universe. I see our multidimensionality. I am aware that at any moment, the unexpected may occur. I know we live in a web of beings, energies, intentions. When we turn a corner on our journey, the vista awaiting us may be breathtaking.

Witches spend time outside the scope of ordinary experience. A tree is not only "a tree."

A tree is an amazing and magical being. A flower is not only "a flower." A flower is a cup of heaven offering nourishment. The ocean is not only "the ocean." The ocean is a massive and energetic being with spirit, a being whose body is home to many others. We see more. We see spirit and life in everything.

※

Vision

I am in a room. I sit in a chair.
It is dark. I see only what is there.
I have been there a long time. I know nothing else.
Just the dark room, the chair, the floor, the walls.
Barren.

Someone comes in.
They are kind. They see me lost.
They walk to the window. Open it.
Sunlight streams in.
A larger world. More possibility. A different story.

They saw the window. They knew there was more.
They opened the window and shared their vision.
They opened my world.

I get up from the chair. I leave the room.

I step into a new story.

Heart Broken

As I tried to recover from Lyme, I worked with various people in various ways. One clairvoyant healer I worked with, Chelsea, focused me on emotional and spiritual healing. Working with her, the memory of losing my childhood pony, Nickel, came up yet again.

When I was maybe eleven years old, I had a baby pony named Nickel – small, rotund, and a beautiful and soft fuzzy gray. He was born on our farm on a cold November day, as it was beginning to snow. I was walking on the road towards our neighbor's house when Dusty, Nickel's mother, whinnied to me from the top of the hill. I raced home because I knew it meant Dusty had her baby. My mother, sister, brothers, and I went to the upper pasture and slowly, step by step, helped tiny newborn Nickel and his mother Dusty get down the hill to the shelter of the barn as the snow thickened and deepened.

I spent my free time with Nickel. Weekends and after school. I taught him to lift his feet. I brushed him. I talked to him. He was my beautiful little friend. One day, I came home from school, and he wasn't there. I looked everywhere, becoming more and more frantic as I realized he was gone. Without telling me, without the chance to say goodbye, my parents had sold him. The people they sold him to came when I was at school, put him in a van, and drove away. No phone number, no address, no way to see if he was safe.

My heart broke that day. Later, as an adult, when I was around thirty years old, I was in a workshop. This memory emerged. I had forgotten. I saw the child who had been betrayed.

That was when I understood more about my depression as a teenager. That was when I began to see more clearly what I had survived and why I was broken.

I have struggled with loss since the beginning of this life. I have held on, not wanting to let go of those who left me or were taken away.

I again experienced the hurt not only of my parents' betrayal but also my loss and my inability to protect this being I loved and adored. My fear that he did not have a good life after he had left our farm. That he had not been loved or cared for. My powerlessness in being unable to hold onto him and care for him.

Saving Who I Could

Where I grew up, farm animals such as horses and ponies outlived their usefulness. They were often taken to the auction and sold to a slaughterhouse. Their days of loyalty betrayed by our inability to take responsibility for those who gave to us their labor, their loyalty, their love, and their lives. I knew what happened at the auctions. I knew the animals were scared. And while some might be purchased and adopted into a good home, many were not. They were crammed into a truck, no food or water and taken away to the slaughter, the smell of blood, the panicked sounds, until they were next. I could not bear this happening to one of the horses or ponies I loved.

This was why, when I went to college, I gave my horse Specks away to a good home. My parents would no longer take care of him or allow him to remain on their property. I wanted him to go to a good home with children where he would be loved.

I could not bear the idea of him terrified, abandoned, and dying in a slaughter assembly line. Rather than sell him, I found him a home in a less rural area with a family that had another horse and kids. I could not save Nickel, but I did my best to save Specks to ensure a happy future for him.

※

Gift

She opened a doorway, a vista, a dream.

She called in hope, grace, possibility,

She showed me a vision I had not imagined.

A weight released, the heralding of dawn.

The Window Opens

Chelsea, the clairvoyant healer I was working with, told me she saw a child who needed Nickel more than I. A child with a disability who needed an animal friend, one that was gentle, sweet, and loving. She told me Nickel was loved and cared for and had changed this child's life. My world turned sideways, and a window opened to a new vision. I had only seen my loss and my inability to protect and care for someone I loved dearly. I had not conceived that Nickel's beautiful presence may have helped someone else.

I do not know if her vision was accurate. Regardless, she opened a possibility that could now stand beside my loss. Perhaps what had happened was not the tragedy I felt it to be. Perhaps there was a higher purpose or gift I had not seen.

Un-Haunted

I do not wish to be deluded. I do not wish to live in fantasy. I want to know the truth. Yet, sometimes, the truth is different according to where we stand. I do not think, as a child, this information would have significantly lessened the blow. I do not even know if this clairvoyant's vision is true. But I hold it as a possibility. As an outcome different from the terrible one that had haunted me for years. That perhaps these stories could stand side by side, and although I did not know for sure which one was truer, I could know that there were more possibilities than I had imagined.

Room to Breathe

When we come from trauma, hurt, and pain, we often do not see the other possibilities. It is hard to find and hold the vision of the positive because we have learned to steel ourselves against what is difficult. This way of being infuses our cells, wraps around us, holds us into a shape that is not our complete unfolding. Learning to imagine other outcomes and knowing that there is often unexpected goodness in the world helps us loosen and find more room to breathe.

I see Nickel in my mind's eye right now. He is long gone from this physical plane, but I see him in a large green grassy field.

I see him happy under the sun, grazing, with a small boy watching him from the fence. Nickel is content. The boy's heart is full as he looks at his furry gray friend.

The miracle of a new vision, a new possibility, a new reality.

Living Journey

You think there is a path.

You think it is logical.

You think there is a map.

A feather falls from the sky.

A bird. A message, perhaps?

A moment to ponder.

Grab onto each magic moment.

Keep walking. The path will emerge.

You will see it unravel behind you.

Ahead, just stardust.

Alive Life

When I became extremely ill in 2009, I didn't know why. I had been pushing myself relentlessly for over two years. I divorced my first husband in 2007 and had been gripped in fear. My body had been ravaged by the stress of that time and the abuse that had been dumped on me. I didn't see how my life was going to fall into place. I couldn't imagine life would cooperate with me, help me. It was as if I believed I had to make everything happen myself. I pushed and pushed myself. I have a strong will and have always been able to make things happen before.

Empty

I gripped onto my will with my fingernails, but I was losing the battle. My will was no match for this disease. There was no life force for me to draw on. Exertion was simply beyond me. I no longer had the physical resources to power my will.

One day, I collapsed. I couldn't push anymore. I didn't have any reserves; I had no physical strength. I had headaches, chills, and nausea. My life had been physical and full. Now, I no longer had the energy for a phone conversation. I went from nearly daily power yoga, weekly hiking, and occasional mountain biking to lying in bed shaking. After even minor exertion, I had to lie down and recover.

I had to be very careful about how I used my energy. Seeing clients was an exercise in will to hold myself up, to get myself through the fifty-minute session, to not show my suffering, my struggle. I laid down for the ten minutes between each session, nauseous and headachy. I once heard it explained like this. You only get ten spoons for each day.

What do you want to use your spoons for? How much gets distributed for each task? But in my case, I only had two spoons. Not enough for a whole life. Not enough even to talk on the phone to a friend.

Seeking

I stopped all strenuous exercise and cut back significantly on my workload. I stopped talking to my friends. I simply didn't have the energy. I began to seek doctors and healers, hoping somebody could help me.

As I saw healer after healer and doctor after doctor, with the medical profession insisting nothing was wrong with me and that perhaps I was imagining it, my hope rose and waned as my illness cycled. But ultimately, I was incapacitated. I could not power my way through my life anymore.

I came face to face with how I had used my will to navigate through my life. If I had wanted to do something, I simply tackled it and did it. But that no longer worked. Instead, I had to learn a new way to move through life. I didn't know what that was. Nor had I yet been knocked entirely to my knees. That would come later as my illness became long-term term, and after another six years had passed, the antibiotics I had been on affected my brain, causing brain fog, desperation, and suicidality.

❋

Life's Decision

It had been as if my will was the center of the universe. To feel safe, I needed to know I could make what I needed to happen. I didn't know any other way. I didn't know how to trust life. I felt alone, that life itself wouldn't be there to assist me.

The need to navigate life using will alone was compelling. And although having a strong will is a valuable skill, it is only part of what is needed to accomplish in the context of a whole and healthy life. My willfulness was too disconnected from the larger currents of life. I was living as if I were a machine. I was not going to be allowed to continue that way. Life had decided this for me – only I didn't know it. It would take years of illness, desperation, even suicidality before I began to understand how to live differently. In this area of life, I could not find my magic.

Made Myself Ill?

It was suggested to me that I had made myself ill. Made myself ill? How? I hadn't been depressed, and I didn't have a bad attitude. What were they talking about? I rejected the blame in that statement then, and I still do. Now, years later, I understand. The pieces that eluded me are becoming visible. Mine was a broader, more profound problem that was spiritual in nature. It had to do with how I understood the world. I wasn't honoring myself fully. I couldn't. But this wasn't conscious. The shifts that needed to occur were built into my path, into the descent I would take with my health. A descent to the underworld of a long-term illness and both the confusion and the soul searching that would initiate. I didn't make myself ill. But the disease that occurred came out of who I was, and moving through it required a re-orientation of myself.

Not honoring another or ourselves can come from many places. It can emerge out of fear or greed. It can come out of a single-minded purpose that makes a goal more important than our significance as beings. It can come out of self-centeredness. In my case, it came from my past. I grew up in a family that was very focused on goals. Doing was supported. Being was not. The honoring of each member of our family was not the focus. Despite the good things I received growing up in my family, our family also had a sickness, a darkness. Perhaps it was my father's darkness – for his need to achieve and his internal struggles overshadowed the spirit of our family. Our internal worlds were not recognized or nurtured.

Crushed

I am giving a tarot reading to a friend. We sit on the rug in my office, cards, and books around us. We explore how she can help one of her friends navigate through a challenge in her life. One of the cards we pull is the Son of Swords in the Mother Peace Tarot deck. This card is the Knight of Swords in a traditional Tarot deck. Later, I pull this card out and look at it more closely. I run my fingers across this card, which I have pulled many times. The image is of a young man. A knight with his helmet. His eyes are focused on an open chest with gold spilling out. In the sky, the sun shines bright. The sun of will. The sun of consciousness.

There is no mystery here, no magic. He cannot see it. The knight wears a violet robe and has his knife drawn, held in his right hand, for he is ready for battle, ready to achieve his will. In his left hand, he holds a dove by the neck. The dove clearly perished; squeezed too hard, her breath stopped.

At his feet lay flowers, unseen. He will step on them, trample them without ever knowing. I have been this person. This person whose eyes are so focused on the supposed goal that the beauty around me and within me is crushed. The journey unseen, for the goal, eclipses the beauty of the present moment.

Journey That Teaches

The journey itself was and is the teacher. Improved health was the outcome. Often, when we set out on a path to get somewhere, it is the journey that teaches, not the place we think we want to get to. For example, I decide to become a therapist. I believe that vocation would be engaging, fulfilling, contribute to the world. And that is true. But it was also a journey where I had to delve more deeply into myself, where I would outgrow my first husband, where I would have to learn to become a fuller, more developed person. Where I would learn to run a business. The journey was the teacher. Becoming a therapist was simply the outline, the sketch that life filled in along the way.

What emerged for me was a new understanding of how the world works. My will is useful when I am correctly aligned with my highest good. But what if we are turned in the wrong direction? What if we've disconnected from the deeper currents of our lives? Sometimes, we hit a dead end, and the only option is to turn around or move in a different direction.

The Journey's Teachings

It wasn't that I was turned in the wrong direction; I just didn't know how to cooperate with other forces. I didn't know how to send a prayer or ask the angels to help me. I didn't know how to feel as if I was being supported by the unseen world around me.

I didn't know how to trust the events of my life or the larger universe. That is what I was to and did learn. It is what I continue to practice.

Synchronicity

I found that I live in a world of synchronicities. When I am off-balance, an event occurs to reflect that off-balance. Perhaps I am moving too fast, not grounded as I prepare a meal and cut my finger on a knife. If I honor myself, the world will also mirror that back to me as well. If I honor others, the world will also reflect that back. Not always in the moment. Not always in a balanced, equal way. But ultimately, who I am creates a field that invites in a reflection of my energy.

Something interesting was happening. I found each piece of my life to be alive. Each person and event has something to teach me, for if I didn't need to learn that piece, it would not be happening. This, of course, is an expansive perspective – like standing far back in the universe and watching the weaving that occurs over eons. It does not diminish or judge the suffering of many caught in compromising situations or treated unfairly. But it does say that the universe interacts with us. Much of what happens is beyond my comprehension, especially suffering, although I believe that we come here to add our light, to learn how to do so, and like an earthworm bringing air into and transforming the dirt, we do the same. Should the dirt be poisonous, the job is much more dangerous and may extract its price from us.

I began to strive to understand more about divine will and the link between divine will and magic. I began to think more about where the line is between myself as a creator being and myself as a co-creator, working with other beings. I began to wonder more about the saying, Thy Will Be Done and what that meant. I began to use the serenity prayer more:

> God Grant Me The Serenity To Accept
> The Things I Cannot Change,
> The Courage To Change The Things I Can,
> And The Wisdom To Know The Difference.

What does all of this mean? It means if I can trust our universe and trust that if I ask for what is in the highest interest of all, I can get out of my own way. I can bypass my blocks, areas where I do not see, and allow the best possibility to manifest. It is knowing that underneath it all, the unseen forces of good have blessed us and want the best for us.

Marvelous Whole

Believing helps living enormously. I choose to believe that which will help me get unstuck and evolve. So, I must trust that the universe contains good forces. I don't know how else to live. To believe otherwise leaves me fearfully crouched in a corner or pushing too hard to compensate for my lack of control.

Life is a living journey that shifts and changes as I grow, offering new challenges, new ways of seeing, and new support. By tuning in, I am no longer in the realm of an isolated will but the realm of relating. When I tune in, when I look at my world with respect and gratitude, I am part of a marvelous whole.

There is a universe within each of us. Within every person or animal, plant, bacterium, or star is a vibrant and bountiful world.

Looking at the outside, we see only the shell, the external form – not the incredible wealth of possibility of that being. Whenever we "use" someone or something without recognizing the universe inside of him or her, we limit the other, our world, and ourselves.

Couples Work

I am working with a couple. We are sitting in my office. The tension in the air is palpable. They are caught. The female partner wants to be loved. The male partner does not know what love is, what he wants, who he wants to love. But he knows he doesn't want to lose his child. His child he loves. Each wants the other to conform to their desires. Each does not fully see who the other is. She cannot see her partner as someone with a steep learning path ahead of him. A path of unraveling a deep sense of being unworthy. A path of releasing escape, fantasy, and addiction to the solid work of loving what is actual and authentic in our lives. She does not see that she cannot make this man different. That she cannot use her will to demand he fit the role she needs him to fill. This is active work for me. I move my focus back and forth between them. Stop them. Slow them down. Ask them to reach deep into their feelings.

"Stop," I say to her one session as she is venting, raging. "Stop." I repeat myself until she stops, breaks her gaze from him, and looks at me. "What are you feeling?" I ask. She looks confused. It takes a moment to reorient to herself. She has been out of her body, caught in a flood of energy, adrenaline.

She answers, "sad, I feel sad." We move down into her sadness, her sense of loss, her impotence to get what she wants. This is the beginning of her enlarging.

Of finding more of herself. Of seeing herself, her loneliness, and the desolation under her rage. And of seeing him more truly, his limitations that he will have to grapple with, rather than seeing only what she needs him to be, what he is not and cannot be.

Dancers in the Sky

When we live in a one-person script, it is as if we are surrounded by cardboard characters put there to serve our every need. We become more limited and less able to access our spirit. The possibility of connection, love, and the recognition of the wonder of each of us is lost. It is our loss and all our losses.

Tuning in allows me to engage with life in an alive way. I am able to experience more of who I am. I become responsive to life, and life responds to me. I engage in the magic of living. It is a very different place to be than living out of one's will.

The living journey demands that we each recognize our role in our journey. We are dancers creating magic as we open our eyes to the deep sky filled with the stars of possibility.

✺

Alive

- full of active power

It is cold. The wind hits me, pushes me. Forceful.
I draw my scarf closer.
I stand my ground, stare into the wind.
My eyes water.
I listen to the trees catch air.
I feel myself part of and separate.
I am alive.

※

Journey of Aliveness

We are alive; every breath, every action, every moment is alive. Every moment, we generate energy — love, hatred, peace, joy, stress, determination, force. We may do this because of or in spite of the conditions around us.

This morning, I drove into town to take a yoga class. I often listen to inspirational podcasts and YouTube when I drive. Today I listened to Abraham Hicks, a group of beings who offer their wisdom and perspectives channeled by Ester Hicks.

As I drove by the lake, the mist was rising. The hills behind the lake were partially cloaked and peeking through the mist. The sun was breaking through the clouds. The water was calm. I felt gratitude for the beauty, the textures, the colors - the muted grays, browns, and greens.

As I appreciated how my drive enabled vistas and visions I would not have seen otherwise, I listened to Abraham explain that the journey is where it is at. This is a message I need to hear because I am often trying to get to the future, and I lose my sense of appreciation and gratefulness for the present.

For me, chasing the future started early. My childhood was filled with yelling, blaming, and resentment. I felt trapped, and I wanted out. Thus began my exit out of the present moment. I moved into my head, into books. I moved into my imagination, into hopes and quests. Difficult experiences were pushed out of my mind. Over time, I became a doer. Being seemed like the stepchild of doing and so I forgot how to be.

Fully Here

I was told once, as I was slogging through a project, that the project was alive, that the energy I was bringing to it would impact how the user experienced it. That stopped me in my tracks. I could no longer show up stressed or half-conscious and push through (although I sometimes still did and do). I had to find a different way to engage. The goal cannot justify a badly lived journey.

As the years flowed by, I meditated, practiced yoga, did creative work, took workshops and training, attended therapy, refined my awareness, and learned to focus on being here right now. I grappled with struggles, relationships, situations, my career, and jobs. At the same time, I lived in a world of feelings: fears, shames, desires, and joys. These feelings add complexity to reality.

Being alive and present means experiencing all of this. Being present is not bliss, but the slow untangling of being with what is while refining how to engage with my consciousness and my reality. This is the magic of being alive.

I don't want to be on my deathbed and wonder what happened to my life. I wish to reside in it fully. I want to see its beauty and wonder. I want to step into the magic of what is possible.

Healing's Magic

How do I do this? How do I experience all of my feelings while also recognizing the unique beauty of each moment and not abuse that moment, not tarnish it because I feel bad, or afraid, or want something else desperately?

Recently, I have been feeling depressed. I felt like a heavy gray fog had settled over me. I couldn't shake it. I brought this up with a healer I work with. She suggested I find the part of me that felt lost, alone, or abandoned and work with that part.

I closed my eyes. I saw a child, grubby with a dirty, raggedy dress. I focused on her. I imagined pouring love into her. After a few minutes, she began to notice the environment around her.

She saw the sky reaching down towards her. She saw the trees were aware of her. She saw the earth holding her. She saw the spirits of her physical environment responding to her. She no longer felt alone, encapsulated in isolation.

When I came out of this inner focus, this pouring of love into a lost part of myself, my depression had lifted. I saw myself more engaged in relationship to all that was around me. Like my shadow connected to my feet, everything was connected to me and responded to me. As I notice and respond to what is around me, what is around me notices and responds to me. This is a place I can revisit. This is the magic of healing.

✶

Perfect Form

Nautilus shell. Galaxy, Sunflower head.
Pine cone. Logarithmic spiral. Golden curve.
Mathematical movement outward.
Embodied being. Intentional form.

I reach my arms outward.
My world. My universe.
Me. You.
Celebrate.
We are here.
Perfect form.

❋

Moment of Grace
It is darkening out and beautiful. The dark descends, and this part of the earth releases a sigh. The night creatures will be stirring, and the day creatures will rest. I feel happy. Perhaps I am finally moving into knowing how to be. Maybe I have let go of the disease of always needing to do do do. Can I imagine a life where I am completely at peace? Where I can fully feel joy? Where I do not have to be headed somewhere to feel safe or okay?

It is as if something too tightly wound is beginning to unwind. It is as if I am okay with my life right now.

It is as if I can see the beauty around me, feel the light on the water and the darkening sky, and at this moment, all is right.

I want to be in a place of acceptance and love for myself and my life. I want to be one of those beings who radiate caring effortlessly. I want to be in full possession of myself and let loose ecstatically at the same time.

Consumed

I don't want to toil and be filled with torturous angst. And yet those times, if I dive down into them, lead me to this time of peace. I dive through the waves rather than get stuck. That is the way, is it not? To stay with each obstruction until the idea of obstruction is no longer valid until it is consumed by the path itself.

Perhaps I get to enjoy who I am. Perhaps I get to like my life. Perhaps my seeking shifts to being.

Thank you, god, thank you, god, thank you, god.

※

Loving My Walk

My work of awareness is ongoing. I can own my journey as something I have power over. I can notice each moment and adjust my course according to what I am experiencing. I can decide to change my path or my attitude. Moment by moment, I can find my connection to what is around me and within me. I can begin the journey of increasing my aliveness in each second. I can integrate the various parts of myself and know I am not alone.

I want to walk that fine razor's edge where I live each moment as beautifully as possible while also respecting the complexity of all my feelings. That is my goal. Loving that walk. Engaging with my present. Finding my gratitude and bringing magic to all parts of me.

✵

Epilogue

Finding Home

The witch flies into the unfathomable black sky.
A sky of stardust, comets, and universes
breathing, pulsing, as she swirls through the air.
She is at home in her flight,
at home in her embodiment.
Connected to the great wild being
that holds us all
she shrieks her delight.

Seeing Each Other

I have a meditation practice where I sit and imagine my divine and physical self in relationship. They witness each other. They honor each other. I bring the ethereal into myself and take in the love of the aspects of me that are not embodied. This enables a process, a connection, an infusing and knowing of these two different aspects of myself. A mirroring occurs where each honors the other. The one doing the hard physical work of embodiment on this planet and the one who provides the inspiration and support from beyond this dimension. Dancing together, they are one.

Claiming my witch self is a part of honoring the feminine and the larger universe. It is part of how I step into my whole multidimensional self.

This book is not over. My journey continues. Book two of *Love's Cauldron* awaits.

The End

Sources
(Selected Bibliography)

Appell, E. *"And the day came when the risk to remain tight in a bud was more painful than the risk it took to blossom."* [Original source disputed; widely attributed to Anaïs Nin.] 1979.

Avelin, D. *Embracing Your Inner Witch: The Maiden's Guide to Old World Witchcraft.* Dark Moon Press, 2016.

Campbell, J. *"Where you stumble and fall, there you will find gold."* [Source unknown.]

Death by Burning. Wikipedia. Retrieved January 22, 2025, from https://en.wikipedia.org/wiki/Death_by_burning

Estés, C. P. *Women Who Run With the Wolves: Myths and Stories of the Wild Woman Archetype.* Ballantine Books, 1992.

Hafiz. *Deepening the Wonder.* Rendered by Daniel Ladinsky. In *The Gift: Poems by Hafiz, the Great Sufi Master.* Penguin Compass, 2000.

Hesse, H. *The Journey to the East.* Holt, Rinehart and Winston, 1956.

Hoffman, A. *Incantation.* Little, Brown and Company, 2006.

Little, T. *Yoga of the Subtle Body: A Guide to the Physical and Energetic Anatomy of Yoga.* Shambhala Publications, 2016.

Niebuhr, R. *The Serenity Prayer.* [n.d.]

Oxford University Press. *Accident.* In *Oxford English Dictionary.* [n.d.]. Retrieved from google.com.

Saint-Exupéry, A. *The Little Prince.* Reynal & Hitchcock, 1943.

Woodman, M. *"The healing of ourselves as healers has to take place first..."* [Source unknown.]

Acknowledgments

Where does one begin with acknowledgments when a book comes from a lifelong journey of developing and healing? There are more to thank than grains of sand.

Thank you to those women brave enough to claim and speak from their witch selves. You have opened space for those who follow in your footsteps.

I want to thank the 12-step groups that helped me understand my limitations and began to heal my anxiety.

Thank you to the many therapists I've had over the years; each helped me to better understand myself and integrate more of myself into a stronger and more solid being.

Nature, Gaia, Our Mother – Our planet provides me with nourishment and peace. Thank you.

Thank you to the great spirits of the cosmos. You, too, have helped enlarge my understanding of our world.

Thank you to my unseen but powerful guidance team. I have relied on you heavily.

Over the years, my many animal friends and pets have helped me better understand the purity of love and have provided much-needed support. I hold all of them in my heart with gratitude.

Without books, I could not have imagined other realities or understood what was possible. Thank you to all the authors who have enriched my world.

I have been a member of many writing groups. Each of these has contributed to me finding my voice and developing my writing ability. Thank you.

Thank you to the esoteric teachers and advisors who have helped me open to understanding more than consensus reality.

Thank you to my dear friends who have supported me on this journey, especially Shelly Eyre Graham, who has been a constant emotional support.

Thank you to the early beta readers of this book. Your input was valued.

Thank you to my editor, Catherine Parnell, my agent, Susan Mears, and my publisher, Chris Day. Each of you contributed to this book's journey.

Thank you to my husband, Michael Bosworth, for supporting my many projects and missions and for his nourishing love.

Thank you to the Web of Becoming that enabled the space for this book to be.

About The Author

"Sometimes, to have a productive and fulfilling life, we first have the task of healing ourselves."
~Jennifer J. Lehr LMFT

Jennifer J Lehr spent years focused this on very task, on healing the parts that were fractured, on finding and integrating the parts of her that were solid. This journey opened her witchy side and love of the feminine. She was compelled to write about her path to a more complete and less fragmented self.

Jennifer holds a certificate in Fine Art from the Pennsylvania Academy of the Fine Arts in Philadelphia. She has a master's in counseling psychology with an emphasis in Depth Psychology from Pacifica Graduate Institute, Montecito, CA.

Jennifer has extensively trained in Gestalt Theory and Therapy, Intersubjectivity, and Emotionally Focused Therapy for Couples and other modalities.

She has been writing her entire life, has run SoulCollage® groups since 2006, and has been a psychotherapist for many years. She founded WeConcile, a relationship growth app, and hosts the Yearning Heart Podcast – where her guests talk about their challenges, learning, and growth in love and relationships.

She previously published a self-help book called The Magic Cake, The Seven Ingredients of a Relationship Ready Person. She has guested on numerous podcasts and written many articles and videos on individual and relationship healing.

Jennifer was born in Red Bank, New Jersey, but has lived on the West Coast for much of her life. She resides on Orcas Island, WA, with her husband and their dog, Nutmeg,

Learn More About Jennifer J Lehr, LMFT

You can find out more about me at Jenniferlehrmft.com.

You can find more out about my podcast, the Yearning Heart Podcast, at
https://weconcile.com/yearning-heart-podcast.

You can also learn about the WeConcile® app at
https://weconcile.com/.

I have numerous videos on my YouTube channels and other social media.

All social links are on my websites.

Image Credit

I would like to thank all those who supported the creation of this book, and acknowledge the sources of visual materials that enriched its pages.

The "Om" or "Unalom" symbol from Cambodia, dated 17 August 2020, was created by *Cambodia Public Domain* and is used here under public domain.

Various icons and images were sourced from The Noun Project under the Unlimited royalty-free license. I gratefully acknowledge the following creators:

madforest
Cattaleeya Thongsriphong
Maria Zamchy
Brad
Gan Khoon
HideMaru
Leonardo Henrique Martini
Lucas Rathgeb
Imogen Oh

These visual contributions helped enrich the storytelling and design of this book.